BARRON'S c Quarter Library

return ti   before the last

TROUBLESOME
WORDS & PHRASES

James E. Allison

*This book is dedicated to my
intrepid wife, Peggy, who kept
the rest of the world at bay during
those times when I desperately
needed to concentrate.*

Copyright © 2000 James Allison

All inquiries should be addressed to:
Barron's Educational Series, Inc.
250 Wireless Boulevard
Hauppauge, NY 11788
http://www.barronseduc.com

Library of Congress Catalog Card No. 00-041357

International Standard Book No. 0-7641-1633-9 ✓

Library of Congress Cataloging in Publication Data
Allison, James E., 1931–
    Quick help with troublesome words and phrases /
by James E. Allison.
        p.   cm.
    Includes bibliographical references.
    ISBN 0-7641-1633-9
    1. English language—Usage—Dictionaries. I. Title.
PE1460 .A56 2001
423'.1—dc21
                                                                00-041357

PRINTED IN THE UNITED STATES OF AMERICA
9 8 7 6 5 4 3 2 1

CONTENTS

Introduction

Although this book was conceived with deadline journalists—copy editors and reporters in the print and broadcast media—and journalism students in mind, it became apparent as it moved along that it had a broader application, that it could be of use to a more diverse segment of the population. So with that in mind, I began to design what I think is a useful tool for students, teachers, writers, ministers, politicians, public relations and advertising people, and businessmen, to name only a few.

In my early years in the news business I relied chiefly on dictionaries and on newspaper style books, which I discovered later were in large part the products of misconceptions and axe-grinding, much of it thrust upon the staff by newsroom personalities long departed.

After I'd been around the block a couple of times, I came to realize there was more to grammar than dictionaries and style books. I discovered Theodore Bernstein's *The Careful Writer,* and it gave me a new perspective on how words are to be used.

I had studied at a small college where I took a major in English and all the journalism courses it had to offer. I can't speak for the big journalism schools then or now, but my little school expected you to use the dictionary and thought you ought to be a better than average speller. But we never got into the finer points of words.

The last newspaper I worked for supplied itself with a few editors just out of the University of Kansas. These young folks came well-prepared and ready to work. It was through them that I became acquainted with a book titled *Words on Words* written by one of their professors, John Brenmer. This was an excellent book on usage, and my understanding is that one of their courses involved reading and discussing the words and phrases Brenmer addressed in his book. These editors didn't appear to be versed in usage much better than those from other schools, but they recognized the importance of proper usage; they always had Brenmer's book close by and never hesitated to use it.

I earned my stripes on copy desks populated by editors who at times would nearly go to blows over the placement of a comma. I haven't seen that kind of enthusiasm on a copy desk in a long time, so that is why it was refreshing to watch the folks from Kansas with their Brenmers at their sides.

I guess that's the way it goes with most of us. There's no way you can commit to memory everything there is to know about words, so life in a newsroom and other places where correct English is important is a constant trip to "the big dictionary" . . . or to a usage book. At least I've burned up my share of shoe leather chasing down the right word.

Once you get to your supply of resources—which may be limited even in the biggest office tower—to look up whatever term is giving you a problem, the first thing you have to do is find a book that discusses it. Not all usage books address all subjects. Once you find what you're looking for, you may have a considerable amount of reading ahead of you before you can determine whether the term is being used properly. Some usage books may spend a page or more on the object of your research. Don't get me wrong—I enjoy reading those books and I read them a lot. But I didn't always have that kind of time to sacrifice to the pursuit of knowledge. These venerable writers provide a history of a word and maybe its etymology. You'll probably read their opinion of it and perhaps that of others. And you may see some funny stories about it. Their mission is to educate and, in some cases, to entertain. Mine is to give you a quick solution.

So all this had been rolling around in my mind for some time, and it occurred to me that I could compile a number of words and phrases that give people the most problems and consult works by a number of usage experts to get an idea of the general feeling toward them. Then I could give a little information about the word or expression and tell you in three or four lines whether you can use it without embarrassing yourself. That would save you a lot of reading. And it would spare you many trips across the room, because these little items would be in a book small enough to keep at your elbow.

I've selected about 1,500 words and expressions. They include look-alike and sound-alike words and cases where conflicting choices exist and some words that are hardly ever spelled correctly. One difficulty I've had is finding the proper preposition for a word, so I provide plenty of those. I also give you lots of examples.

I consulted the works of the authors mentioned on the next page, as well as the more recent desk dictionaries. Because many of my favorite word books were written long ago, I put a lot of weight on the usage notes in the dictionaries, especially in cases where there appeared to be a significant shift in the prevailing attitude toward a particular usage. I learned that many words that were taboo when I was a pup have achieved respectability over the years.

So what I've tried to do is give you a book with the most up-to-date information available in a form that will save you time. If you care about how words fit into your sentences, then this book is for you.

Jim Allison
January 2001

Bibliography

I consulted works by many of the leading authorities on English usage and five of the most recent desk dictionaries to determine the current status of the words and expressions that I deal with in this book. Because many of the more respected usage guides were written a number of years ago, the dictionaries' usage notes were considered carefully.

These are the dictionaries that were principally used.

The American Heritage Dictionary, Second College Edition, 1985
The Concise Oxford Dictionary of Current English, Ninth Edition, 1995
Merriam Webster's Collegiate Dictionary, Tenth Edition, 1993
Random House Webster's College Dictionary, 1992
Webster's New World Dictionary of American English, Third College Edition, 1988

Also used:

The Oxford American Dictionary, 1980
The Oxford Universal Dictionary, 1933, revised 1955
Fowler's Concise English Dictionary, 1911, revised 1989

Usage books consulted:

The ABC of Style, A Guide to Plain English by Rudolf Flesch, 1964
The American Heritage Book of English Usage, 1996
American Usage and Style, The Consensus by Roy H. Copperud, 1980
The Associated Press Stylebook and Libel Manual
The Careful Writer, A Modern Guide to English Usage by Theodore M. Bernstein, 1965
Comfortable Words by Bergen Evans, 1962
The Dictionary of Cliches by James Rogers, 1985
A Dictionary of Contemporary American Usage by Bergen Evans and Cornelia Evans, 1957
A Dictionary of Modern English Usage by H.W. Fowler, Second Edition, revised by Sir Ernest Gowers, 1965
Dictionary of Problem Words and Expressions by Harry Shaw, 1975
Edwin Newman on Language (*Strictly Speaking*, 1974 and *A Civil Tongue*, 1975)

The Elements of Style, third edition by William Strunk Jr. and E.B. White, 1979

Funk & Wagnalls Standard Handbook of Synonyms, Antonyms, and Prepositions by James C. Fernald, 1947

Get It Right! by John B. Opdycke, 1935

The Handbook of Good English by Edward D. Johnson, 1991

Harper Dictionary of Contemporary Usage by William and Mary Morris, 1975

An Index to English by Porter G. Perrin, fourth edition, revised by Karl W. Dykema and Wilma R. Ebbitt, 1965

Loose Cannons and Red Herrings by Robert Claiborne, 1988

Mark My Words, A Guide to Modern Usage and Expression by John Baker Opdycke, 1949

Miss Thistlebottom's Hobgoblins by Theodore M. Bernstein, 1971

Modern American Usage by Wilson Follett, 1966

Modern English Handbook by Robert M. Gorrell and Charlton Laird, 1962

Modern Guide to Synonyms and Related Words by S. I. Hayakawa, Funk & Wagnalls, 1968

The New York Times Manual of Style and Usage, 1976

Saying What You Mean by Robert Claiborne, 1986

Smaller Slang Dictionary by Eric Partridge, 1961

Watch Your Language by Theodore M. Bernstein, 1958

Webster's Dictionary of English Usage, 1989

What's the Good Word? by William Safire, 1982

Words on Words by John B. Brenmer, 1980

Coming to Terms

The labels that dictionaries use to classify usage levels of words are sometimes misleading.

For example, when something is labeled *colloquial* or *informal*, a lot of people think they'll be banished from polite society if they use it. That isn't what is meant. In this book, when I say dictionaries consider a word *colloquial* or *informal*, I mean that there's nothing wrong with using it in conversation. The makers of dictionaries usually have a *conversational style* of writing in mind when they use these two words. Sometimes I use *casual* to describe this type of usage. This means an expression is all right for the corner tavern or over lunch, but you wouldn't want to carry it to a higher level.

Dictionaries and many usage writers use the term *formal*. A couple of my dictionaries say that *formal* applies to language of an impersonal or official nature and is characterized by strict adherence to standards of correctness, expanded vocabulary, and complete and complex sentences. Such language is free of contractions and colloquial expressions. This doesn't quite lay it out in black and white, but it helps. You and I are concerned with *words*, and as I view this description of *formal*, words that the dictionaries consider *standard*—those presented without comment, without a classifying label, or without a note of warning—are the words that should be used.

I don't use *formal* very often, but I do use the phrase *serious speech or writing* quite a bit. What I refer to here is usage you would expect to find in a newspaper or a television newscast ("not recommended for serious speech or writing," or "acceptable in serious speech or writing"). This creates a category that is a shade below *formal* in which *standard* words and expressions are used, and I think this is the level on which most of us want to work. So if I neglect to tell you otherwise, assume that we're on this level.

Dialectal and *regional* mean that an expression is found principally in a certain geographical area. For example, I'm comfortable using *you-all* conversationally in Louisville, Kentucky, or Tifton, Georgia, but it wouldn't fly in New York or Chicago or San Francisco. Most words and phrases in these categories are not recommended for *serious* speech and writing.

When I say a particular word is *preferred*, I mean most of my dictionaries list that word or phrase before its alternatives and it is the choice of most commentators. That doesn't mean the other term is incorrect.

If I describe a word as *acceptable*, that means that the word is treated as *standard* by most of my usage guides and dictionaries.

Commentators and *authorities* are people who have written definitive books about proper word usage. *Usage guides* are books written by commentators and authorities.

When the entry word (or words) or a derivative is used in the term's description, it is printed in *italics*. When a term that is described elsewhere in this book (a cross-reference) is mentioned, it appears in SMALL CAPITALS. Phrases and sentences cited as examples are enclosed in parentheses.

A

abhorrence, abhorrent The noun *abhorrence* (a feeling of repugnance or loathing) takes the preposition *of* (my *abhorrence* of their lifestyle). *Abhorrent*, an adjective meaning detestable, loathsome, is followed by *to*. The idea was *abhorrent* to their principles.

ability, capacity *Capacity* is innate; *ability* may be innate or acquired (*capacity* to learn to sing; *ability* to hit the long ball). See CAPACITY.

ability to *Ability* is followed by an infinitive rather than a gerund. (He has the *ability* to pull rabbits out of a hat. Wrong: the *ability* of pulling rabbits out of a hat.)

abjure, adjure *Abjure* means to solemnly forswear, renounce, repudiate. (They *abjured* their allegiance to the king.) *Adjure* means to charge, command, or entreat solemnly or earnestly, often under oath or threat of penalty. (The judge *adjured* the defendant to give up his wicked ways.)

–able a suffix meaning fit for, capable or worthy of, or tending, given, or liable to that is attached to verbs to create adjectives such as debatable, perishable, blamable, manageable, laudable.

abolition, abolishment *Abolition* is preferred.

aboveboard one word.

abrasions, lacerations, contusions medical terms for scrapes, cuts, and bruises.

a cappella This is the correct spelling.

accept, except The similarity in sounds is occasionally the source of confusion between these two verbs. *Accept* means to receive, to agree with. (Smith *accepted* the trophy.) To *except* is to omit, exempt, exclude. (Harry was *excepted* from the physical education class until his foot healed.) See EXCEPT.

access usually followed by the preposition *to*. (We have *access* to the company's financial records.)

accidentally, accidently The correct spelling is *accidentally*; sometimes mispronounced *accidently* and misspelled the same way.

He was prone to accidents.

accident, mishap An *accident* is an unforeseen, unintended occurrence that can be fortunate or unfortunate, minor or major (a lucky *accident*; a fatal *accident*.) A *mishap* is an unfortunate accident. (I sprained my thumb in a bicycle *mishap*.) A number of usage commentators would restrict *mishap* to minor occurrences, but this is not supported by most dictionaries.

accommodation often misspelled.

accordion not *accordian*.

accusation See RECRIMINATION, ACCUSATION.

accuse, charge A person is *accused of* or *charged with* a crime. (The clerk was *accused of* theft. The butler was *charged with* murder.) See CHARGE, INDICT, ARRAIGN.

accused, suspected Avoid calling a person an *accused* murderer, *accused* thief, *accused* rapist, etc. (Jones, the *accused* murderer). It may carry the implication that the person actually is a murderer or thief. The same applies to *suspected*. See SUSPECT.

acknowledgment not *acknowledgement*, except in British English.

A.D., B.C. *A.D.* stands for *anno Domini* (in the year of the Lord). Use before a year, as in *A.D. 71. B.C.—Before Christ*—is used after the year (*15 B.C.*). (The document covers the period from 50 B.C. to A.D. 50.) *B.C.E.*—Before Christian (or Common) Era—and C.E.—Christian (or Common) Era—are appearing more and more frequently.

adage An *adage* is an old saying. Therefore, several usage commentators advise us that it's redundant to refer to an old *adage*.

adapt, adopt To *adapt* is to adjust or modify to make suitable for a specified use or situation. To *adopt* is to choose and use as one's own. (The school board *adopted* a revised set of rules. The teachers *adapted* to the new procedures.) See ADOPTED, ADOPTIVE.

adapted, suitable *Adapted* means adjusted to requirements or conditions. It should not be used as a synonym for *suitable*, which means appropriate, acceptable, fitting. See SUITABLE.

addendum, addenda The plural *addenda* is preferred to *addendums*, although *addendums* is not wrong.

adduce, deduce *Adduce* means to cite as evidence. (He *adduced* three books as proof of his position.) *Deduce* means to reach a conclusion by reasoning. (We *deduced* from his criminal history and comments made by his friends that he was prone to violence.)

adjacent, contiguous. The distinction here is that while *contiguous* means touching, in contact with, *adjacent* means next to, nearby. But something *adjacent* may also touch. We toured the 48 *contiguous* states. The garage was *adjacent* to the house.)

adjure See ABJURE, ADJURE.

admissible *-ible* occasionally misspelled.

admission, admittance *Admission* may be used in all senses, but *admittance* is restricted to the physical act of entering or being let in. *Admission* carries with it certain rights and privileges that *admittance* does not. (They were allowed *admittance* to the clubhouse but were denied *admission* to the club.) Also, "price of *admission*," "*admission* of guilt."

admit to You *confess to* or *admit* something, not *admit to* it, a number of usage authorities say. But most recent desk dictionaries treat *admit to* as standard. (The clerk *admitted to* cooking the books.)

ad nauseam to a sickening, disgusting degree. (The speech dragged on *ad nauseam*.) Frequently misspelled *ad nauseum*.

adopted, adoptive A child who has been *adopted* is called an *adopted child*. Those who adopt the child are called *adoptive parents*. (The *adopted* children found happiness with their *adoptive* parents.) See ADAPT, ADOPT.

adrenalin, adrenaline   *Adrenaline* (epinephrine) is a secretion of the adrenal glands. *Adrenalin* is a trademark for synthetic or chemically extracted forms of epinephrine. (The hard-fought game kept the *adrenaline* flowing.)

advance, advanced   As an adjective, *advance* means in front (*advance* party of soldiers) or beforehand, ahead of time (*advance* payment). *Advanced* means at a higher level than others (*advanced* chemistry, *advanced* weaponry) or far on in life (an *advanced* age).

advance, advancement   *Advance* indicates forward movement, progress (the army's *advance*). *Advancement* means promotion, furtherance. (His elevation to CEO of the subsidiary was a major *advancement*. The foundation contributed $1 million for the *advancement* of science.)

adverse, averse   *Adverse* means unfavorable to or opposed to, hostile. (He suffered from *adverse* publicity. The prevailing mood was *adverse* to his cause. The *adverse* mood damaged his cause.) *Averse* is reluctant, opposed, disinclined. (I'm *averse* to lending money to strangers.) Both words usually take the preposition *to*. See AVERSE, AVERSION.

advert, avert   *Advert to* is to turn attention to, refer to. (The committee chairman *adverted* to the financial report.) To *avert* is to turn away or prevent. (He slammed on his brakes to *avert* a collision.) See AVERT, AVOID.

advice, advise   *Advice* is a noun; *advise* is a verb.

advisedly   To do something *advisedly* is to do it after careful consideration, deliberately. (He and I speak *advisedly*.)

affect, effect   *Affect* means to act on, to influence, to have an effect on. (The strong wind *affected* the golfer's swing.) *Effect* as a verb means to bring about, to accomplish, to execute, to cause. (The mediator *effected* a settlement. As a noun, *effect* means result, consequence, accomplishment.

affinity   *Affinity* refers to a liking for or attraction to a person or thing. Its usual prepositions are *to, between, with,* and *for* (John's *affinity to* Joan, John's *affinity with* Joan, the *affinity between* John and Joan, John's *affinity for* politics).

afflict   See INFLICT, AFFLICT.

aftermath   originally applied to a second crop, such as grass, growing after an earlier mowing. It is now used chiefly for unpleasant results or consequences after a disastrous event (the *aftermath* of war, the *aftermath* of the storm).

afterward, afterwards *Afterward* is preferred.

agenda   Treat *agenda* as a singular. (An ambitious *agenda* was approved.) Its plural is *agendas*. Although *agendum* is not incorrect as the singular, it is rarely used.

aggravate   *Aggravate* means to make a bad condition worse. (The rainy weather *aggravated* his cold.) It is used informally to mean annoy, irritate.

agnostic, atheist   An *atheist* denies the existence of God; an *agnostic* believes it is impossible to know whether God exists.

ago, since   You may say, "It's been 20 years *since* we left Chicago" or "We left Chicago 20 years *ago*," but not "It was 20 years *ago since* we left Chicago." In the last example, *ago* should be followed by *that*.

agree   followed by the preposition *to* (*agree to* the terms) or infinitive (*agree to* go), *with* (*agree with* me), *on* (*agree on* the details), or a clause (*agree* that they would share the cost).

ahold   *Ahold* is considered informal and is used mostly in speech. It means hold or grasp or (get) in touch with. It is followed by *of*. (Take *ahold of* my hand. I tried to get *ahold* of Mom but the line was busy.)

aide   a person who serves as an assistant. Do not write it *aid*.

aim   *Aim* followed by an infinitive is acceptable. (We *aim* to win the championship.) So is *aim* followed by *at* (We *aim* at winning the championship.) but that is not quite so widely used.

air   *Air* is considered acceptable as a verb meaning to broadcast, as on radio or television. (The segment will *air* Friday night.)

airfare   one word.

albeit   a conjunction meaning although, even if, notwithstanding. Considered archaic earlier this century, it is now in fairly common use. (The partnership was profitable, *albeit* brief.)

alibi   *Alibi* means elsewhere in Latin. In law, it means proof that a defendant was not at the scene of the crime he is accused of committing. (The jury accepted the defendant's *alibi*—that he was out of town when the crime was committed.) By extension, *alibi* is used for excuse, especially one that involves an attempt to avoid blame. (His *alibi* for being late was that he had a flat tire.)

alien   most often takes the preposition *to* in the sense of opposed, hostile, strange. (The requirements of the job were *alien to* his principles.)

align   *Align* is preferred to *aline*.

all-American   This construction is accepted by most recent dictionaries for noun and adjective.

all but one   When *all but one* is followed by a noun, the verb is singular. (*All but one* book was sold.) Inserting *of the* makes the verb plural. (*All but one of the* books were sold.)

alleged   Avoid applying *alleged* to persons; it should be used for actions or things; as in *alleged* murder, not *alleged* murderer. Also, watch where you place it: the *alleged* report of extortion should read the report of *alleged* extortion.

all of   Some authorities consider *of* superflous when the phrase is followed by a noun. (*All of* the clerks [all the clerks]), but it would not be wrong to keep it. However, *of* should remain when it is followed by a pronoun (all of us, all of them).

all ready, already   *All ready* means completely prepared. (They were *all ready* to go.) *Already* means before, previously, as early as, as soon as, by this time, before the time in question. (We *already* have that model. Our friends had *already* arrived.)

all right, alright   Use *all right*, not *alright*.

all together, altogether   *Altogether* means completely, wholly, in all. (You are *altogether* wrong. There were six of us *altogether*.) *All together* means everyone in one place at the same time. (We were *all together* to discuss our strategy.)

all told   everything considered, in all. The numerical sense (*all told*, 150 people worked on the project) is used more widely than the general sense. (*All told*, it was a dull experience.)

allude, refer   To *refer* is to mention specifically and directly. (He *referred* to the court order.) To *allude* is to mention something indirectly, without naming it. (He apparently was *alluding* to Jack's infidelity.)

ally   usually followed by *to* (*Allied to* this issue is the question of money.), or *with* (England was *allied with* France.), and sometimes *against* (England and the United States were *allied against* Germany and Italy.).

almost   used infrequently as an adjective modifying a noun (an *almost* stop, an *almost* accident, an *almost* failure).

almost, most   *Most* is widely used informally for *almost* in certain cases: with pronouns such as all, anyone (most anyone), with adjectives all, any and every (*most* any day), and adverbs such as everywhere and anywhere (*most* anywhere): This usage appears chiefly in speech.

almost never   *Almost* appears frequently before negatives such as never, no, and nothing (found *almost* nothing, was *almost never* bored).

alongside of   *Alongside of* is an acceptable idiom that means at the side of. The *of* is dispensable. (The cutter pulled *alongside* our boat.)

along with   See TOGETHER WITH.

aloof   usually takes the preposition *from*. (They remained *aloof* from the little town's squabbles.)

already   See ALL READY, ALREADY.

alright   See ALLRIGHT, ALRIGHT.

altar, alter   An *altar* is a place where religious rites are performed. To *alter* is to change.

alternate The verb *alternate* is followed by *with* (Rain *alternated* with sunshine.) or *between* (We *alternated* between Chicago and Pittsburgh.) It usually applies to only two persons or things.

alternately, alternatively *Alternately* means one after the other. (They *alternately* walked and ran.) *Alternatively* means one or the other. (If you don't drive, *alternatively*, you could take the train.)

alternative An *alternative* is a choice between two or more possibilities. (The bus runs till midnight. Your only *alternative* is to walk.)

altogether See ALL TOGETHER, ALTOGETHER.

alumnus Forms for graduates or former students of a school: *alumnus*, masculine singular; *alumna*, feminine singular; *alumnae*, feminine plural; *alumni*, plural for males or a group composed of both sexes.

A.M., P.M. Both may be capitalized but they are seen more often in lowercase and small caps. They stand for *post meridiem* (after noon) and *ante meridiem* (before noon).

amateur, novice An *amateur* is one who engages in a pursuit, such as art, just for the pleasure of it, with a lack of skill implied. In sports, an *amateur* is an athlete who participates without pay, regardless of the level of skill. A *novice* is a beginner, whether amateur or professional.

ambience, ambiance Both spellings are accepted. The word refers to the environment, surroundings, distinct atmosphere or mood of a place, thing, or person (the cafe's delightful *ambience*). The adjective is *ambient*.

ambiguous, equivocal *Ambiguous* describes language subject to more than one interpretation. (They were confused by the report's *ambiguous* summation.) The ambiguity may be intentional or unintentional. *Equivocal* applies to something that is deliberately ambiguous. (The prisoners parried their captors' questions with *equivocal* replies.)

ambivalence, ambivalent *Ambivalence* is a simultaneous conflicting or contradictory feeling, such as love and hate, toward a person or thing. Its adjective is *ambivalent*. (He talked about the stormy relationship he had with his parents and the resulting *ambivalence* he felt toward them.)

amend, emend   *Amend* is to improve, modify, correct, change, or revise (a legislative bill, law, constitution, etc., as well as written material). *Emend* is a more specialized term that applies to corrections or improvements in text, mainly literary or scholarly works.

American   *American* is accepted by recent dictionaries and many usage guides for a resident of the United States and for something pertaining to the United States. *America* is an acceptable synonym for the United States.

America's Cup   proper form for the yacht race.

amiable, amicable   *Amiable* describes a friendly, likable person or persons (an *amiable* clerk not easily upset), *amicable* is characterized by good will, a showing of friendliness (an *amicable* settlement, an *amicable* discussion).

amid, among   Although these words are often used interchangeably, *among* is preferable for things that are separable, and *amid* as being in the middle of things that are not necessarily countable (walking *among* the trees, keeping cool *amid* the confusion).

amok, amuck   Either spelling is acceptable, although *amok* may be the slight preference (running *amok*).

among   See AMID, AMONG.

among, between   *Between* usually applies to two persons or things, *among* to three or more. (It was a choice *between* Jones and Smith. The winnings were divided *among* five players.) However, *between* is used with three or more items that are considered individually (talks *between* Germany, England, and France).

amoral, immoral   An *amoral* person is unaware of or does not care about society's moral standards; an *immoral* person is aware of the standards but disregards them.

amount, number   *Amount* refers to bulk, mass, or sum (an *amount* of money, an *amount* of time). *Number* refers to countable nouns (a *number* of days, a *number* of errors).

ample, enough   *Enough* is an amount sufficient to satisfy a requirement or need. (We had *enough* money to pay the rent.) *Ample* means enough to fulfill a need with room to spare. (The supply of food was *ample*—easily sufficient to last through the winter.)

Amtrak   not *Amtrack.* It's an acronym that comes from (*Am*)erican (*tra*)vel by trac(*k*).

amuck   See AMOK, AMUCK.

anachronism   an error in chronology in which a person, object, event, custom, etc., is represented as existing or occurring at other than the proper historical time; something that appears to be out of its proper time, such as Benedict Arnold faxing top secret documents to the British. *Anomaly* and *paradox* are sometimes misused for *anachronism.* An *anomaly* is a deviation from the normal or common order, form, or rule. A *paradox* is a statement that seems contradictory but may in fact be true, or someone or something that seems to have contradictory qualities.

analogous   similar, alike. It uses the preposition *to* in most cases. (My situation is *analogous* to Charlie's.) Also takes *with*, but infrequently.

and/or   sometimes unnecessary. *And* or *or* will often suffice.

and that   When you have a second clause introduced by *and that*, for the sake of parallelism you must also use *that* in front of the first clause. (The investigator said *that* the fire started in the basement and *that* it appeared to be arson.)

angry   You are angry *at* or *with* a person (I was *angry at/with* the clerk.), *at* or *about* a thing. (I was *angry about/at* their snub.) See MAD, ANGRY.

antenna   The plural is *antennas* for radio and television aerials, *antennae* for insects.

anxious, eager   *Anxious* and *eager* both indicate keen desire, but *anxious* implies an uneasiness, an apprehension that *eager* does not (*anxious* to close the deal before something else went wrong, *anxious* about his physical, *eager* to start the game, *eager* to see his parents). See EAGER.

any   *Any* is acceptable when used as an adverb meaning *at all* to modify a comparative adjective. (Is she *any* better?) It is informal or colloquial when used in that sense after a verb. (If he whines *any*, tell his mom.)

anybody, anyone   Technically, these words use singular verbs and singular masculine pronouns. (If *anyone* wants to leave, he may use the side door.) Many people object to the masculine pronoun, so sometimes you see plural pronouns. I prefer to recast the sentence. (*Anyone* who wants to leave may use the side door.) See EVERYBODY, EVERYONE.

anymore   now, any longer, at present. It is used in negative statements (They don't drink there *anymore*.), negative connotations (I hardly see them *anymore*.), or questions. (Do you see movies *anymore*?) Do not use in affirmative constructions: (I go to the gym twice a week *anymore*.) Either one or two words—*anymore* or *any more*—is acceptable, though one word is used most often.

anyplace   *anywhere* preferred as adverb. *Anyplace* is often used in conversation and sometimes in writing, but it should be avoided in serious speech and writing.

anyway   one word as an adverb meaning nevertheless, in any case, regardless. (It may rain, but we'll go to the game *anyway*.) Two words are used to mean in any manner. (Do it *any way* you can.)

apathy   Its preposition is *toward* (showed *apathy* toward their plight).

apology, excuse   An *apology* is an acknowledgment of error or discourtesy and an expression of regret (He offered an *apology* for his rude conduct the night before.) An *excuse* is an explanation offered to justify a fault or to deflect blame. (Her *excuse* for missing the start of the meeting was heavy traffic.) See EXCUSE.

apparent, evident   Both apply to something readily understood and easily perceived. *Apparent* involves a conclusion reached by deductive reasoning, and *evident* a conclusion supported by visible signs. (As the lead mounted, it was *apparent* that he would win. It was *evident* that a struggle had occurred.)

appendix   *Appendixes* is the plural form more widely used to refer to supplementary material that usually appears at the end of a book or other piece of writing. *Appendices* is not incorrect and is often used in scholarly writing.

apportion   Followed by *among, to,* and *between* (*apportioned among* the states, *apportioned to* each school according to its need, *apportioned between* the two cities).

appraise, apprise   To *appraise* is to set a price on, to establish the quality or importance of (having your property *appraised*, *appraising* the candidates). To *apprise* is to notify, to inform. (The committee was *apprised* of today's developments.)

apprehensive   In the sense of fearful, anxious, it usually takes the preposition *for* when applied to persons (*apprehensive for* their friend, who was two hours late) and *of* when referring to things (*apprehensive of* speeding cars). Sometimes it is followed by *about* (*apprehensive about* my opponent's next move) or a clause (*apprehensive* that we may not get the loan).

apprise   See APPRAISE, APPRISE.

apt, liable, likely   *Apt* and *likely* are used interchangeably for inclined, tending to, expected, or probably. (I'm *apt* to change my mind. It's *likely* to rain today.) *Liable* applies to what is unpleasant or undesirable. (They are *liable* to regret their decision to take a vacation at this time.)

arbitrator, mediator   An *arbitrator* hears evidence from opposing parties, then hands down a binding decision. A *mediator* hears arguments from both sides in a dispute, then attempts to help them reach a solution. A *mediator* does not dictate a settlement.

archetype   sometimes misspelled, as *archtype*.

archive, archives   The plural form is more widely used. (The *archives* in the county courthouse have been moved to a new location.) The singular form sometimes appears (a living *archive*).

area, field   Either word is often unnecessary when used in the sense "She earned three awards in the *field* [or *area*] of education." Make it "...three awards in education."

argot, jargon   *Argot* is a specialized or secret vocabulary used by a particular group for private communication and identification (thieves' *argot*). *Jargon* is the specialized terminology of a trade, profession, or similar group (medical *jargon*).

arguable, arguably   *Arguable* means open to argument, supported by argument. It can be used in a positive, negative, or neutral sense. (Whether Jack is the best person for the job is *arguable*.) *Arguably* is used mostly in a positive sense. It means "it can be *argued* that" or "as can be supported by *argument*" (*arguably* the best third baseman in the league).

around   See ROUND, AROUND.

arraign   See CHARGE, INDICT, ARRAIGN.

aroma   pleasant odor. It should not be used to describe a disagreeable smell except facetiously.

artisan, artist   *Artist* is applied chiefly to a person skilled in one of the fine or performing arts—a painter, a sculptor, a singer, or actor. An *artisan* is a person skilled in an art or craft that requires manual dexterity—a woodworker or a potter, for example.

as far as   The omission of the verb in the clause that this phrase introduces is considered poor usage. Wrong: *As far as* the budget, the council may have to increase taxes. This should read, *As far as* the budget is concerned....

as follows   (The club listed the winners as *follows*.) Not *as follow*. Idiom dictates that you use the singular *as follows* even though the subject and verb preceding it are plural.

as if, as though   These two phrases are used interchangeably, but the subjunctive is used with both. (The child looked *as if* [or *as though*] she were [not was] near tears.)

ashamed   takes prepositions *of, for*, or *to*. *Of* is used most often. *For* is used when you feel shame that someone else should be feeling. *To* is used with the infinitive (*ashamed* of myself, *ashamed* of our project, *ashamed* for our team's display of poor sportsmanship, *ashamed* to read my essay to the class).

Asian, Asiatic, Oriental   *Asiatic* and *Oriental* are considered offensive in most uses as noun and adjective. Use *Asian.*

aspiration   The preposition used most often is *for* (*aspiration* for justice). Sometimes it's *of* followed by a gerund (*aspirations of* becoming a star) or *to* followed by a noun or infinitive (*aspirations to* become a star, *aspirations* to stardom).

aspire   Its chief preposition is *to* followed by a noun or an infinitive. (She *aspired to* the presidency. He *aspired to* become president.) *After* and *toward* are sometimes found.

assay, essay   As verbs, *assay* means to test, to analyze; *essay* means to attempt. As nouns, *assay* means test; *essay* means an attempt or a short literary effort. (The chemist *assayed* the pieces of metal. Will you *essay* this project? Your *essay* was delightful reading.)

assent   The verb is followed by the preposition *to* (*assented to* their proposal, *assented to* their viewpoint).

assess   to set a value on for purposes of taxation or to impose a tax, fine, etc. (The county *assessed* my property at $150,000.) *Assess* also means to judge the significance, importance, or value of, evaluate. (Let's *assess* our chances.) It does not mean to charge someone with a foul or penalty. Do not say "A foul was *assessed* against the Wildcats" or "The judge *assessed* a five-year sentence."

assume, presume   In the sense of suppose or take for granted, these two terms are roughly interchangeable, with *presume* based on a stronger belief in the probability of something and an absence of evidence against it, and *assume* merely venturing a hypothesis. (I *presume* this check is good. Let us *assume* their intentions are honorable.)

as to   This phrase is standard English, although often it should be replaced with a more precise preposition. (There was some doubt *as to* [about] their qualifications.) However, it's handy for pulling something you want to emphasize up to the front of the sentence. (*As to* taxes, the committee saw no reason to suggest an increase.)

as well as   See TOGETHER WITH.

at about   *At* is usually superfluous. (The bus arrived about 3 P.M. Wrong: at about 3 P.M.)

atheist   See AGNOSTIC, ATHEIST.

attorney general   Plural is *attorneys general.*

attorney, lawyer   Technically, a *lawyer* is an *attorney* only when he or she is representing a client. But *attorney* is frequently used for *lawyer*, and many *lawyers* refer to themselves as *attorneys.* A *lawyer* is a person who is qualified to practice law; an *attorney* is someone who is empowered to represent another. An *attorney* does not have to be a lawyer, though he or she usually is. (She acted as *attorney* for her incapacitated sister.)

auger, augur   To *augur* is to foretell the future by interpreting signs and omens. (This *augurs* well for our plans.) Often misspelled *auger*, which is a boring tool. (The worker made holes in the door with an *auger.*)

augment   Its preposition is usually *by.* (Some teachers *augment* their salary *by* tutoring.) Sometimes *with* is used. (She *augmented* her pay *with* a job as a tutor.)

The sudden appearance of a small dark cloud did not augur well for their little picnic.

au naturel   often misspelled *au natural.* It means in the natural state (naked, for example) or cooked or served plainly or simply.

author, authoress   As a transitive verb, *author* is treated as standard by recent desk dictionaries but generally discouraged by usage commentators. (She *authored* five books.) It is most readily accepted when the creation is by more than one person, such as a committee. (The finance committee *authored* the bill.) *Coauthor* as a verb encounters no such problems. *Authoress* should be avoided.

avenge, vengeance, revenge   Although *avenge* and *revenge* are often used interchangeably, there is a distinction worth observing. To *avenge* is to exact retribution for a wrong done to someone other than the avenger. (The two brothers *avenged* the humiliation of their sister.) Its noun is *vengeance.* To *revenge* is to get even for something that someone did to the revenger. (The team *revenged* its embarrassing defeat.) *Revenge* is also the noun.

average, mean, median An *average* is the total of a group of figures divided by their number. A *mean* is the middle point between two extremes. A *median* is the point in a group of numbers at which half the numbers are above it and half below it. Using the numbers 2, 3, 6, 9, 12, the *average* is 6.4, the *mean* is 7, and the *median* is 6. *Mean* is sometimes used as *average*.

averse, aversion Both forms are most frequently followed by *to* (*averse* to joining the club; an *aversion* to work). See ADVERSE. AVERSE.

avert, avoid *Avert* means to prevent or to ward off. (The driver's quick reaction *averted* a collision.) To *avoid* is to shun, keep clear of. (He went to the store early to *avoid* long lines at the checkout counter.) See ADVERT, AVERT.

avocation, vocation Your *vocation* is your occupation. (My *vocation* is nursing.) Your *avocation* is your hobby. (My *avocation* is flying kites.)

await, wait Both are used as transitive verbs (to *await* [*wait*] your orders, to *wait* [*await*] your turn), but *await* is not ordinarily used intransitively. See WAIT FOR, WAIT ON.

awful, awfully *Awful* originally meant inspiring awe, causing fear (the *awful* responsibility). It is now used for unpleasant, disagreeable, horrible, terrible (an *awful* attitude, *awful* manners). The use of *awful* and *awfully* to mean very, great, or extremely (*awfully* pleased) is informal.

awhile, a while *While* is a noun; *awhile* is an adverb, not used after a preposition. (He stopped for *a while*. He stopped *awhile*.)

AWOL *absent without leave*, especially from military duties.

B

baby boom, baby boomer   usually lowercase.

back of, in back of   Both phrases are acceptable. (There was a shed *back of* [*in back of*] the house.)

backward, backwards   Either form is acceptable as an adverb, but *backward* appears to be preferred. Use only *backward* as an adjective. (The car was moving backward. He gave her a *backward* glance.)

bacteria   plural of *bacterium*, a word that is rarely seen.

bad, badly   Use *bad* rather than *badly* when the word follows a copulative verb such as to be, appear, become, feel, look, seem, smell, or sound. (I feel *bad*. You look *bad*. The team looked *bad*. But: The team played *badly*.)

badly (very much)   *Badly* in the sense of very much or greatly is standard. (They want it *badly*. The house is *badly* in need of repair.)

bail, bale   You *bail out* a boat and *bail* a prisoner out of jail. You *bail out* of a difficult situation; you *bail* a friend out of a difficult situation; you *bail out* of an airplane. When you *bale* something, such as hay, you make it into bundles, usually compressed and bound.

balance   Although the use of *balance* in the sense of rest or remainder is not incorrect, its usage in this sense has many critics. In strict usage, it applies to the difference between debit and credit and should not be used for rest or remainder except when two amounts are involved. (I gave him five of the ten dollars and kept the *balance*.) Such uses as "the *balance* of the day was spent shopping" are discouraged. Rest or remainder are recommended in these contexts.

balding   May be used as an adjective: "the thin, balding professor."

baloney, bologna   The sausage is *bologna* (a pound of *bologna*). The slang term for nonsense is *baloney*. (The lawyer said the charge against his client was baloney.) Sometimes the sausage is called *baloney*, a variant generally considered informal.

barbecue   This spelling is preferred to *barbeque*, *Bar-B-Que*, and *Bar-B-Q*.

barbiturate   frequently misspelled and pronounced *barbituate*.

bated breath   It's not *with baited breath* when you're holding your breath in suspenseful anticipation of something; it's *bated*.

bathos   *Bathos* means a ludicrous change from the exalted to the commonplace; anticlimax. It also applies to overdone or grossly sentimental pathos. Its adjective is *bathetic*. *Bathos* is used mostly by literary critics.

bazaar, bizarre   These two similar-sounding words have completely different meanings. A *bazaar* is a Middle Eastern market or a fund-raising fair or sale. *Bizarre* means odd, strange, unusual. (The club's *bazaar* was *bizarre*.)

B.C.   See A.D., B.C.

bear, born, borne   The past participles of *bear* when birth is involved are *borne* and *born*. *Borne* is used when speaking of the mother and it is preceded by *has* or followed by *by*. (Two sons were *borne by* her. She has *borne* two sons.) When *born* is used, it is in the passive and the focus is on the child. (I was *born* on the Fourth of July. The twins were *born* forty-five minutes apart.) *Borne* is used in all other senses.

She was beat after getting beaten by a younger foe.

beat, beaten   *Beat* is the past tense. *Beat* and *beaten* are the participles. *Beat* is informal for tired out or exhausted, or in reference to a movement of youths who rebelled against convention in the 1950s (the *beat* generation). *Beaten* is the adjective in all other senses (*beat* after a hard day's work, the *beaten* path, *beaten* to a pulp).

because   See DUE TO, BECAUSE.

beg the question   This phrase is often misused to mean raise a question or to dodge the issue. It means to assume the truth of the very thing being debated, like citing God's perfection in a discussion about whether He exists.

behalf   In strict usage, *in behalf of* means for the benefit of or in the interest of, and *on behalf of* means as an agent of or in place of. (The club raised money in *behalf* of the orphanage. The attorney filed a motion on *behalf* of his client.) The phrases are often used interchangeably and this is accepted by most current dictionaries.

beholden   This word was once a participle of *behold*, which means to gaze at, observe, see. It survives as an adjective meaning to be obliged, indebted, its only meaning. It takes the preposition *to* (*beholden to* no one).

belittle, disparage   Both mean to make something seem little or less important than it appears. *Disparage*, in addition, means to reproach, degrade, discredit.

bellwether   not *bellweather*. It means someone who takes the initiative or something that indicates a trend. It originally meant a male sheep, usually wearing a bell, that leads the flock.

bemuse   A person *bemused* is muddled, bewildered, stupefied, confused, or lost in thought (*bemused* by the complexities of the judicial system). It is not synonymous with *amuse*.

bereaved, bereft   Both of these words are past participles. *Bereaved* applies to the death of a loved one, and *bereft* the deprivation or lack of something. Both take the preposition *of* (*bereaved* of my mother, *bereft* of their senses).

beseeched, besought   Either *beseeched* or *besought* is correct for the past tense and past participle, but *besought* appears far more often. To *beseech* is to entreat, implore, beg for, or request earnestly or urgently.

beside, besides   *Beside* means at the side of. (They stood *beside* the judge.) *Besides* means in addition to, other than, except. (Three people *besides* me were in the room.) See TOGETHER WITH.

besought   See BESEECHED, BESOUGHT.

bestow   *Bestow* is usually followed by *on* or *upon*. (Many honors were *bestowed* upon the research team.)

bet, betted   *Bet* is the past tense and past participle of choice for *bet*, although the rarely used *betted* is not incorrect.

bête noire   sometimes spelled *bête noir*, which is incorrect. It is something or someone that is feared or disliked, a bugbear. Its plural is *bêtes noires*.

better than   acceptable for "more than." (We drove *better than* 500 miles today.)

between   See AMONG, BETWEEN.

between you and me   not "between you and I." Also: "*between* them and us" and "*between* him and her."

biannual, biennial   *Biannual*, like *semiannual*, means twice a year. *Biennial* means every two years.

bimonthly, semimonthly   *Bimonthly* means both every other month and twice a month, creating considerable confusion. *Semimonthly* has only one meaning—twice a month. If the context cannot be made clear, use "every other month" or "twice a month" instead of *bimonthly*.

bipartisan, partisan   *Partisan* applies to an adherent or supporter (a strongly *partisan* Republican). *Bipartisan* means supported by, character-ized by, or involving two parties or factions. (The bill received *bipartisan* support as the two parties set aside their differences.)

bit, bitten   Both are acceptable as past participles of *bite*, but *bitten* appears more frequently. (I'd been *bitten* by the scheme before.) The past tense is *bit*.

biweekly, semiweekly   *Biweekly* is another two-headed *bi-* word. It means every two weeks or twice a week. Make sure your context is clear. (A short-age of news forced the newspaper to switch from a weekly to *biweekly* oper-ation.) There's no problem with *semiweekly*, which means twice a week. (The *semiweekly* newsletter appears on Tuesdays and Fridays.)

bizarre   See BAZAAR, BIZARRE.

blame   *Blame for* and *blame on* both are standard. (They *blamed* the mistake *on* me. They *blamed* me *for* the mistake.)

blatant, flagrant   *Blatant* means offensively loud and boisterous, clamorous, brazenly obvious, offensively conspicuous (a *blatant* attempt to intimidate the witness). *Flagrant* means glaringly bad, notorious, outrageous (a *flagrant* violation of the ethics code).

blindman's buff   sometimes called *blindman's bluff*, which is considered incorrect by some usage authorities but is accepted by most current dictionaries.

bloc   a coalition of people, groups, or nations united for a particular purpose (the farm *bloc*, the coffee *bloc*, the European *bloc*). Do not use *block* when you mean *bloc*.

blond, blonde   The adjective for both men and women is usually *blond*, although *blonde* is sometimes used for women. The nouns are *blonde* or *blond* for women, and only *blond* for men.

boat, ship   Generally, a *boat* is described as a small craft propelled by oars, sails, or a motor, and a *ship* as a large oceangoing vessel propelled by sails or engines. Boat is sometimes used to refer to the larger vessel in casual conversation, but you would be wise to observe the distinction in serious speech and writing (or in the presence of anyone who has ever served in the U.S. Navy).

bogey, bogy, bogie   *Bogey* is a golf score of one stroke over par on a hole. All three spellings are used to refer to a hobgoblin, although *bogy* is preferred. *Bogey* also is used for an unidentified aircraft. The usual plurals are *bogeys* for *bogey*, and *bogies* for *bogy*.

bona fide   two words.

born, borne   See BEAR, BORN, BORNE.

breach, breech   *Breach* is a violation or infraction, as of a law, faith, legal obligation, or promise (*breach* of promise, *breach* of contract) or a gap or rift made in a solid structure such as a wall, fortification, or dike. (There was a *breach* in the dam. The invaders poured through a *breach* in the west wall of the fort.) *Breech* is the rear part of the bore of a firearm

bridle path   a trail for riding horses. *Bridal path* is incorrect.

bring, take   *Bring* indicates movement toward the speaker; *take* indicates movement away from something or someone.

Briton, Britisher, Englishman *Briton* is preferred to *Britisher* in reference to a resident of the British Isles. If he's an *Englishman*, call him an *Englishman*; if she's a *Scotswoman,* call her a *Scotswoman.* Dictionaries label *Brit* informal or colloquial. See SCOT, SCOTTISH, SCOTCH.

broadcasted *Broadcast* is favored over *broadcasted* as the past tense and past participle of *broadcast.*

brunet, brunette *Brunet* is the usual noun for boys and men, *brunette* for girls and women. *Brunet* is the most common adjective for both sexes. *Brunet* also is used as a noun for girls and women, but not as frequently as *brunette.*

bug In the sense of electronic eavesdropping, *bug* is acceptable as a noun and a verb. (The *bug* was found in a vase. They *bugged* the judge's chambers.)

burglary, robbery, theft *Burglary* is stealing someone's property by means of breaking and entering. *Robbery* is taking something by violence or threat of violence. *Theft* is larceny that does not involve violence or breaking and entering.

"Your father is the best bronco-busting buckaroo in the state of Delaware."

burned, burnt Both forms are correct for the past tense and past participle of *burn.* *Burned* is more common in the United States; *burnt* is the preference in Great Britain.

bust *Bust* is not acceptable as a verb meaning *burst* or *arrest.* It is accepted as a verb meaning to *break* (as a bronco, or a trust) and to *demote.*

C

cactus   Its plural is usually *cacti. Cactuses* is not incorrect; *cactus* is seen infrequently as a plural.

Caesarean section   This is the preferred construction. *Cesarean* is also accepted.

calculate   To *calculate* is to determine by mathematical methods, reasoning, or evaluating. (We *calculated* that our supplies would run out in February.) It is considered dialectal when used as a synonym for think, guess, suppose, or intend.

callous, callus   *Callus* is a noun and is used as a verb meaning "causing calluses." *Callous* is an adjective meaning "having calluses, insensitive and unfeeling," and a verb meaning "to become hard or insensitive." *Callused* and *calloused* are interchangeable when they describe the skin condition. Only *callous* can be used in the figurative sense (a *callous* attitude).

calvary, cavalry   *Calvary* is the place near Jerusalem where Jesus Christ was crucified. *Cavalry* is a unit of troops on horseback.

candelabra, candelabrum   In strict usage, the preferred singular is *candelabrum* and its plural is *candelabra*. Also acceptable are *candelabra* as a singular and *candelabras* as its plural and *candelabrums* as the plural of *candelabrum*.

can, may   Although these words are often used interchangeably, mostly in informal speech, *can* properly denotes capability and *may* permission. (I *can* cross my eyes. You *may* leave now.)

cannon   The plural is *cannon* or *cannons*. (The *cannon* [or *cannons*] were taking a heavy toll on the enemy positions)

cannot   standard as one word or two, but *cannot* is the heavy preference.

cannot help but   Despite criticism from many quarters that it forms a double negative, this phrase enjoys widespread acceptance, as do *cannot* *but* and *cannot help*. (I *cannot help but* laugh when I think of it. I *cannot but* laugh… I *cannot help* laughing…)

canvas, canvass   *Canvas* is a coarse cloth. (The tent's *canvas* was showing wear.) *Canvass* is to solicit votes, opinions, sales orders, etc., or to inspect votes. (The candidate's staff *canvassed* the neighborhood. The loser demanded a *canvass* of the votes.)

capacity   Followed by *to* and an infinitive (their *capacity to* survive), *for* and a noun (*capacity for* love), *for* and a gerund (my *capacity for learning*), *of* when it refers to volume (a *capacity of* 30 tons), and *as* or *of* when it refers to role or position (in my *capacity as* host). See ABILITY, CAPACITY.

capital, capitol   A *capital* is the city where a state or nation's seat of government is located. A *capitol* is the building where a legislative body meets. (Tallahassee is the *capital* of Florida. Congress meets on *Capitol* Hill.)

carat, karat, caret   *Carat* is a unit of weight for precious stones. *Karat* is a unit for measuring the fineness of gold. *Caret* is a mark to indicate where written or printed material, such as a letter or a word, should be inserted.

casket, coffin   When used to refer to the box in which a body is buried, these two words are interchangeable. But technically, *coffin* is the burial box and *casket* a small chest or box, as for jewels.

casualty   This originally meant only an *accident*. It has been extended to military personnel killed, wounded, captured, or missing in action. (The regiment's *casualties* rose steadily.) It can also mean victims of disaster, such as a traffic accident, plane crash, storm, earthquake, etc. (Authorities released a list of *casualties* in the train-bus collision.)

catalog, catalogue   Both may be used, but *catalog* is the favorite.

catastrophe, catastrophes   These forms are correct. They are sometimes misspelled *catastrophy* and *catastrophies*.

cater-cornered   *Cater-cornered* is preferred for diagonally (*cater-cornered* across the street). *Cater-corner* is also acceptable. Popular variants are *catty-cornered* and *kitty-cornered* (or *catty-corner* and *kitty-corner*).

caution Its preposition is usually *against* (*cautioned* them *against* discussing the plan) and less frequently *about* (*cautioned* them *about* talking too much). Also used with infinitive (*cautioned* them *to cross* at the intersection).

celebrant, celebrator A *celebrant* is a person who officiates at a religious rite, such as mass. A *celebrator* is one who participates in festivity, merrymaking, revelry. However, *celebrant* is often used, not incorrectly, for *celebrator*.

cement, concrete *Cement* is a mixture used to make *concrete*. (The house was built with *concrete* blocks. The building firm needed more *cement* for its *concrete* mixture.) *Cement* is sometimes used informally for *concrete* (the *cement* sidewalk).

censor, censure To *censor* is to suppress or delete content from material such as books and movies. To *censure* is to criticize or rebuke in a harsh manner. (Mail was *censored* during World War II. The congressional committee recommended that their colleague be *censured*.)

center around *Center on*—or *upon, at*, or *in*—is generally favored over *center around* or *about*, although *center around* has a handful of defenders among recent dictionaries and usage commentators who consider it idiom. Workable alternatives to *center around* include revolve around or swirl, hover, cluster, rotate around. (The police investigation *centered on* [revolved around] the black car.)

century See MILLENNIUM.

ceremonial, ceremonious *Ceremonial* means pertaining to ceremony and applies to things (*ceremonial* robes). *Ceremonious* applies to people and things and means full of ceremony, excessively formal (a *ceremonious* entrance). When *ceremonious* refers to people it means pompous, ostentatious, overpolite, punctilious.

chafe, chaff To *chafe* is to wear away by rubbing, abrade, to make sore by rubbing. (The starched collar *chafed* my neck.) It can also mean to heat or make warm by rubbing or to irritate, annoy, vex. (The criticism *chafed* him.) To *chaff* is to banter, to tease good-naturedly. (They *chaffed* the bridegroom at the bachelor's party.)

He chased her around
the chaise longue.

chaise longue   not *chaise lounge* or *chase lounge*. Its plural is *chaise longues* or *chaises longues*.

chance The verb *chance* is followed by *on* or *upon*. (We *chanced* upon a wreck.) It can also be followed by an infinitive. (We *chanced to find* my lost watch.) The noun's most common preposition is *of* (*chance* of success) and, in various contexts, *at, for,* and *on* (had a *chance* at it, took a *chance on* finding them at home, our last *chance for* victory).

chaperon, chaperone Either spelling is correct, but *chaperon* predominates.

charge, indict, arraign   To *charge* is to accuse formally of a crime; to *indict* is to find sufficient evidence to warrant a trial, an action usually taken by a grand jury; to *arraign* is to call before a court to answer charges. (The police *charged* them with arson last week and they will be *arraigned* today. They were *indicted* by the grand jury yesterday.) See ACCUSE, CHARGE.

chief justice   The proper title of the presiding justice of the U.S. Supreme Court is *chief justice of the United States*.

childish, childlike   *Childish* takes on an unfavorable sense when it refers to an adult (her *childish* behavior, his *childish* remarks). *Childlike* suggests favorable characteristics (*childlike* innocence, *childlike* faith). *Childish* is the word to apply to children, not *childlike*. (*Childish* laughter came from the playground.)

children   plural of *child*. The plural possessive is *children's*.

chili, chile   *Chili* is preferred, though *chile* is often used and is standard (*chili* con carne, *chili* sauce, *chili* dogs). The country in South America is *Chile*.

choral, chorale   *Choral* is an adjective that means "of or pertaining to a chorus or choir." *Chorale* is a noun that applies to a hymn or a group that specializes in singing sacred music. It is used infrequently as a synonym of *chorus* or *choir*.

chord, cord   A *chord* is a combination of musical notes. *Cord* is the proper spelling for a rope or string and is used in such constructions as spinal *cord*, vocal *cords*, and umbilical *cord*.

circumstances   uses the prepositions *in* or *under*. (They lived *in* comfortable *circumstances*. The performance was adequate *under* the *circumstances*.)

cite   See SIGHT, SITE, CITE.

civilian   describes a person who is not an active member of the armed forces or a police or firefighting agency. (The police were assisted by a group of *civilians*.)

clamber, clamor   *Clamber* is a verb that means to climb awkwardly, using both feet and hands. (They *clambered* across the rolling ship's deck.) *Clamor* is a noun and verb that pertains to a loud uproar, an expression of discontent or protest. (The zoning plan brought a *clamor* from nearby residents. The group *clamored* for better roads.)

clean, cleanse   *Cleanse* is used primarily in a figurative sense (*cleansed* of sin, *cleansed* my soul), while *clean* is used in a more literal sense (*cleaned* their rifles). *Cleanse* is used chiefly with the preposition *of* (*cleansed of* guilt). It is not incorrect to use it in the literal sense to mean *clean*.

clench, clinch   Both mean to secure a nail, a screw, etc., by flattening the protruding point. But in other senses, *clench* means to close hands, teeth, etc., tightly (*clenched* my teeth), and *clinch* means to settle something decisively—to *clinch* a deal, agreement, etc. (We *clinched* the Willoughby contract.)

client   See PATRON, CUSTOMER, CLIENT.

climactic, climatic   *Climatic* refers to the climate. (I liked the *climatic* conditions in Florida.) *Climactic* involves a climax. (The diving catch by the shortstop in the ninth inning was the *climactic* play.)

clinch   See CLENCH, CLINCH.

close proximity   usually redundant. It's often better to use *close, near,* or *proximity*. (My *close proximity* [*proximity*] to the office saved money on gas. Our home was in *close proximity* to [*near* or *close to*] the expressway.)

cloture   This is the technical term for a parliamentary procedure for cutting off debate on a matter before a legislative body and taking a vote. (The Senate invoked *cloture* to end the long filisbuster.) *Closure* is also used frequently in this sense, apparently with the approval of some dictionaries but against the advice of most usage authorities.

coffin   See CASKET.

cohort   Originally a Roman military unit, *cohort* now is often used for companion, colleague, associate, or accomplice, but this use is criticized by usage commentators, and most dictionaries advise against using it. It probably should be avoided except in informal contests.

coiffeur, coiffure   *Coiffure* is a French word that refers to the manner in which hair is arranged, and a *coiffeur* is a male hairdresser. A female hairdresser is a *coiffeuse*.

coleslaw   almost always one word; not *cold slaw*. *Cole slaw*, two words, is not wrong.

collaborationist, collaborator   *Collaborationists* are those who cooperate with an enemy occupying their country, a definition shared with *collaborator*. (They were accused of being *collaborationists* during the German occupation.) A *collaborator* is also one who works with someone in a joint artistic, literary, or scientific project. (Rodgers was Hart's *collaborator* on the musical.) *Collaborationist* is not used in this sense.

collide   A *collision* occurs between two moving objects; for example, a moving vehicle cannot collide with a parked car. (The car jumped the curb and *collided* with a wall [struck a wall]. The car crossed the median and *collided* with a northbound truck.)

collusion   a secret agreement between two or more persons for fraudulent or deceitful purposes. It shouldn't be used for cooperation, collaboration, or concert. (Police suspected *collusion* between the cashier and the robber.)

comma fault   the use of a comma, rather than semicolon, colon, or period, between related main clauses not connected by a conjunction. (The speaker paused, she reached for a glass of water.) Also called a *comma splice*.

commensurate   usually followed by *with* (a salary *commensurate with* their accomplishments).

commingle   correct spelling. It means to mix together. (The board was upset when it discovered its treasurer's funds had been *commingled* with the company's.)

commiserate   The usual form is intransitive followed by *with*. (We *commiserated with* her over her loss.)

commitment   no double *t*.

common   See MUTUAL, COMMON.

compare, contrast   To *compare* is to examine for likenesses and dissimilarities, and to *contrast* is to show only differences. (We *compared* Sally's report with Harry's. The study *contrasted* life in the inner city with life in the suburbs.) The verb *contrast* is followed by *with*. The noun form uses "*contrast* between" and "in *contrast* to." See CONTRAST.

compare to, compare with   *Compare to* is used when a similarity is observed between two persons or objects. (They *compared* the rookie's style *to* DiMaggio's.) *Compare with* is used when two persons or objects are put together to examine similarities and differences. (The report *compared* Cincinnati *with* Cleveland.)

compendious, compendium   *Compendious* means containing the essentials of a subject, usually a comprehensive one, in a concise form. A *compendium* is a brief summary of a larger work, an abstract, and its plural is *compendiums* or *compendia*. (The administration released a *compendious* report on its achievements.)

complacent, complaisant   *Complacent* means self-satisfied, *complaisant* showing a desire to please. (The team became *complacent* after the string of victories. The investors found the zoning board quite *complaisant*.)

complected   Although it is widely used where *complexioned* is meant, *complected* is still considered informal and ought to be avoided in serious speech or writing. (The *dark-complected* stranger should read *dark-complexioned*.)

complement, compliment   *Complement* is something that fills out, makes complete, makes perfect. *Compliment* is an expression of praise or courtesy. (The pin *complements* her dress. We *complimented* the couple on their party.)

comprehensible, comprehensive   *Comprehensible* means capable of being understood, intelligible. *Comprehensive* means large in scope or content, inclusive. (This summary is barely *comprehensible*. A *comprehensive* discussion of the issues.)

comprise   consist of, to contain. (The department *comprises* five divisions.) It is frequently used passively in the sense of *compose* or *make up*. (The department is *comprised* of five divisions.) However, this use has gained little acceptance.

comptroller, controller   Use *comptroller* for a financial officer of some governments, such as the *U.S. comptroller of the currency*, and *controller* for the financial officer of a business.

concern   The noun *concern* is followed chiefly by the prepositions *for, over,* and *about* (*concern for* the environment, *concern over* our friend's problem, *concern about* my health).

concerned   In the sense of anxious or troubled, *concerned* commonly uses the prepositions *for* and *about* (*concerned for* his safety, *concerned about* sales). It also takes *over, at,* and *by* (*concerned over* their slow progress, *concerned at* the public mood, *concerned by* the persistent pain).

The cardinals selected a new pope at the conclave.

conclave   a private or secret meeting, especially a meeting of Roman Catholic cardinals secluded while selecting a new pope.

concrete   See CEMENT, CONCRETE.

confidant, confidante, confident   A *confidant* is a person to whom secrets are told or with whom private matters are discussed. It may refer to either sex, though it is primarily used as masculine. *Confidante* is the female noun. *Confident* is an adjective that means having confidence, full of assurance.

conformity   takes prepositions *with* or *to*. (The board demanded *conformity to* regulations. I acted in *conformity with* my parents' principles.)

congenial   Its preposition is *to* (a cafe *congenial to* our tastes).

congenial, genial   *Genial* means sympathetic, cheerful, cordial (*genial* host, *genial* disposition). *Congenial* means similar in spirit and temperament, compatible (a *congenial* group).

congressman, congresswoman   a member of the U.S. Congress, especially the House of Representatives. (The *congresswoman* scheduled a number of appearances in her district.)

connect   usually is followed by *to* when it means to link or fasten in a literal sense, and *with* when used in a figurative sense meaning to relate or associate (*connected* the jack *to* the phone, *connected* their ideas *with* mine). *With* is sometimes used in the literal sense but use of *to* in the figurative sense is rare.

connive   to wink at or close your eyes to wrongdoing, thus giving tacit cooperation. (Police *connived* to allow prostitution in their district.) Some dictionaries allow *connive* as a synonym of *conspire*, but most commentators frown on this use of *connive*.

connote, denote   To *denote* is to express the explicit meaning. (The word "father" *denotes* male parent.) *Connote* is to suggest or imply or signify. (To me, spring *connotes* a period of change, a new beginning.)

consensus   general agreement, collective opinion. "Consensus of opinion" and "general consensus" are usually redundant. (The committee's *consensus* was that the project should proceed.) Often incorrectly spelled *concensus*.

consequent   uses the prepositions *on* or *upon* (the silence *consequent on* the teacher's order to shut up) and, less often, *to*.

considerable   large or great, a lot of. It usually applies to immaterial things (a *considerable* time, *considerable* attention). It does not work well with material things (*considerable* cars, *considerable* paint.) In these constructions, try "a considerable number of " or "a considerable amount of."

consist of, consist in   *Consist of* means to be composed of or to be made up of. (The house *consists of* six rooms.) *Consist in* means to be contained, to reside, to lie in. (His charm *consists in* his soft-spoken manner.)

consonant   an adjective that means consistent, in accord, in harmony and is followed by the preposition *with* (a decision *consonant with* his principles).

contact   Its use as a verb meaning "to communicate with" is opposed by a number of usage experts, but it is treated as standard in most current desk dictionaries. If you'd feel comfortable with a more specific term try call, write, speak to, meet with, call upon. *Contact* is a handy term when you're not sure of the means of communication.

contagious, infectious   A *contagious* disease (such as influenza) is transmitted by contact. An *infectious* disease (such as typhoid fever) is spread by water or air.

contemporary   When *contemporary* is used during discussion of something in the past, it must refer to what was contemporary at that time, not the present time. When there is no connection with the past, *contemporary* refers to the present.

contemptible, contemptuous   *Contemptible* means deserving contempt. (The drunk's behavior in the restaurant was *contemptible*.) *Contemptuous* means showing contempt. (The board was *contemptuous* in its handling of the complaint.)

content, contents   *Contents* is what is contained in something (*contents* of the jar, table of *contents*). *Content* applies to the meaning or significance of a speech or work of art or a literary work (the *content* of the dissertation) or to an amount (high fat *content*).

contiguous   See ADJACENT, CONTIGUOUS.

continual, continuous   *Continual* means occurring repeatedly over a long time with periodic interruptions. *Continuous* means steady, without interruption (*continual* phone calls, eight hours of *continuous* rain).

contrast   used to show differences between two things. Both noun and verb may use prepositions *to* or *with* (*contrasting* life in New York City *with* life in Peoria). The noun sometimes takes *between* (the *contrast between* New York City and Peoria). See COMPARE, CONTRAST.

controller See COMPTROLLER, CONTROLLER.

contusions See ABRASIONS, LACERATIONS, CONTUSIONS.

conversant familiar or acquainted (with) as a result of study or use. It takes the preposition *with* (*conversant with* local history).

convict usually followed by *of* (*convicted of* murder) and in some cases *by* (*convicted by* their own mistakes).

convince, persuade You *convince* someone that something is correct, and you *persuade* someone *to* take a course of action. *Convince* takes the prepositions *of* or *that*, but not *to*. (They *convinced* the couple *that* they should leave. They *persuaded* the couple *to* leave.)

cop an informal term often used, sometimes in a derogatory sense, for police officer. Not recommended for serious writing or speaking

cope to contend with a situation, problem, or a person. (He's having trouble *coping* with the higher rent. I can't *cope* with that child.) Its preposition is *with*, but it is often used without a preposition. (We could no longer *cope*.) Usage commentators and recent dictionaries are divided over the use of *cope* without *with*.

copyright *Copyright* is a noun (obtained a *copyright* for his novel), an adjective (a *copyright* story) and a verb. (They *copyrighted* the story.)

cord See CHORD, CORD.

corespondent a third party accused of committing adultery with the defendant in a divorce action. Often misspelled *correspondent*. It is occasionally used with a hyphen (*co-respondent*).

correspond In the sense of in harmony, agreement, *correspond* takes the prepositions *to* or *with*, preferably *with*. (Our version *corresponds with* theirs.) In the sense of to be analogous or similar, it takes *to*. (The functions of a parliament *correspond to* those of Congress.)

could of   See SHOULD OF.

council, counsel   A *council* is a deliberative body (town council, student council). *Counsel* is advice. A member of a *council* is a *councilor* (town councilor); one who gives advice is a *counselor* (marriage counselor, camp counselor). In law, *counsel* refers to legal advice (entitled to *counsel* at the state's expense) or advisors (Would *counsel* approach the bench?). Lawyers are sometimes called *counselors*.

country, nation   These words are correctly used interchangeably, but in strict usage *nation* applies to a community of people, a political entity (a *nation* in turmoil), and *country* refers to a nation's territory (an enormous *country*). But you should say, "I'm loyal to my *country*."

couple   You'll save yourself a lot of grief if you treat it as plural, avoiding the following type of construction. "The *couple* got married two years after it went into business together and it bought a house in the suburbs. It was divorced last year." This sounds better with plural verbs, plural pronouns.

couple of   *Of* is necessary in such phrases as "A *couple of* cars were sold." Note the plural verb. Omit *of* before *more* or *less*. (I need a *couple* more dollars.)

court-martial   The plural is *courts-martial*. Verb forms are *court-martialed, court-martialing*.

Court of St. James's   The British royal court. Note the apostrophe *s*.

crass   unrefined, gross, stupid, insensitive, indelicate, or coarse. (The antics of the *crass* group at the next table ruined our evening.) It is used to mean cheap, mercenary, or greedy.

crayfish   This construction is preferred to *crawfish* or *crawdad*, which is considered dialectal.

credible, creditable, credulous   *Credible* means believable (a *credible* witness). *Creditable* means deserving of honor or esteem (a *creditable* performance). *Credulous* means willing to believe too readily, gullible (*credulous* acceptance of the salesman's claims).

creep   *Crept* is the past tense and past participle.

crescendo   The proper meaning is a gradual increase in volume in a musical passage or any increase in force or intensity. *Crescendo* is often applied to a climax or peak reached from such an increase, but this is not considered correct. The preferred plural is *crescendos*, although *crescendi* is not wrong.

crisis   Its plural is *crises.*

crisscross   frequently misspelled (with a hyphen).

criteria   Its singular is *criterion.* Proper constructions are *criteria are* and *criterion is,* but not *criteria is. Criterions* is not wrong as the plural, though it is not often used.

critique   accepted as a verb by most current dictionaries. It means to discuss, review, analyze, or evaluate critically. (The committee *critiqued* our project.)

cue, queue   *Cue* applies to the theater (a signal for an actor to do something) and to billiards (the stick you hit the ball with). *Queue* refers to a line of people or a pigtail, though *cue* sometimes is used in place of *queue* in these senses. The word applying to storage of computer data is *queue.* (The gunshot was the actor's *cue* to enter. The line *queued* out the door onto the street. The third player chalked his *cue* while he waited his turn. The computer operator checked her miscellaneous *queue.*)

The actors waited in queue for their cue.

culminate   to reach the highest or climactic point or degree. Its main preposition in its intransitive sense is *in.* (The campaign *culminated* in a narrow victory.) The transitive sense is also acceptable. (The treaty *culminated* seven years of fighting.)

cupful   The plural is *cupfuls.* See -FUL.

curriculum   Its plural is *curricula. Curriculums* is acceptable but not widely used.

customer   See PATRON, CUSTOMER, CLIENT.

D

dastardly A *dastardly* act is one that is cowardly and sneaky, mean, treacherous, or vicious. An element of cowardice must be present. (Jesse James was killed in a *dastardly* attack, shot in the back while straightening a picture in his home.)

data In strict usage, *data* is the plural of *datum* and takes plural verbs, modifiers, and pronouns. However, it is now widely used as a singular, and such usage is standard. (This *data* proves my point.)

daylight saving time This is the accepted form, rather than *savings time*. Its use with a hyphen—*daylight-saving time*—is also proper. *Saving* is usually dropped when a specific time zone is used (Eastern *daylight* time). This construction is frequently capitalized (*Eastern Daylight Time*).

dead body usually redundant. Delete *dead*. (The *body* was discovered at sunrise.)

deal When *deal* means to concern oneself or itself or to take action, it takes the preposition *with*. (The class *deals with* art appreciation. I'll *deal with* that problem.) When it involves selling, the preposition is *in* (*dealing in* used cars). *Dealt* is the past tense and past participle.

debar, disbar To *debar* means to exclude, shut out, hinder, prevent; its preposition is *from*. (People without passes were *debarred from* the meeting.) To *disbar* means to expel from the legal profession. (The lawyer was *disbarred* for stealing from his clients.)

debut The use of *debut* as a verb is disparaged by a number of usage authorities but is acceptable to most current dictionaries intransitively. (She'll *debut* in *The Nutcracker*.) It can also be a transitive verb. (The auto companies will *debut* their new models next month.)

decimate The word originally meant to kill one in ten members of a military unit as a punishment inflicted by Roman commanders for mutiny or cowardice. It is now accepted for destruction of a large part of

36

a group. (Famine *decimated* the population. Drought *decimated* the herd.) Don't use with a fraction or a percentage, such as "Famine decimated half the population."

deduce See ADDUCE, DEDUCE.

defect usually followed by the preposition *in* (a *defect in* hearing, a *defect in* their operation).

defective, deficient *Defective* is faulty, having a defect (a *defective* clutch). *Deficient* is insufficient, inadequate in amount or degree. (The food supply was *deficient*.)

defend uses prepositions *against* and *from* (*defended* himself *against* the charges, *defended* the book *from* criticism).

defenestrate to throw a person or thing out the window. It is rarely used but is accepted by most dictionaries and I find no outcry from usage commentators. (The new concepts covered in the course required the students to *defenestrate* many old ideas. I was on the verge of *defenestrating* the balky computer.) All my desk dictionaries accept the noun *defenestration*.

deficient When it needs a preposition it takes *in* (*deficient in* common sense, *deficient in* calcium). See DEFECTIVE, DEFICIENT.

definite, definitive *Definite* means clear and precise. *Definitive* means final, beyond challenge. "A *definite* starting time" is one that is explicit. "A *definitive* plan" is one that is not open to debate.

deism, theism *Deism* is a belief in the existence of a god based on reason rather than supernatural relevation. *Theism* is a belief in the existence of a creator and ruler of the universe, based on supernatural revelation.

delay, postpone Both words mean to put off until later, but *delay* also can mean impede or hinder. *Postpone* carries the implication that what was put off will be followed up. (Rain *delayed* the start of the game. The meeting was *postponed* and probably will be rescheduled for Thursday.)

delusion, illusion An *illusion* is a false perception, perhaps created by a magician's trick. A *delusion* is a false belief, firmly fixed in the mind. (Harry

is under the *delusion* that his mother is still alive. The three-D movie created some scary *illusions*.)

demand   Its prepositions are *for, on* (or *upon*), or *of*, used according to the
context (*demand for* doctors, *demand for* gasoline, *demands on* my time, the
demands of my job).

demean   There are two *demean* verbs. One, the older, usually reflexive,
means to conduct or behave oneself in a given manner. (They *demeaned*
themselves the way that was expected.) It is now seen only rarely. The other
verb means to lower in status, character, or dignity, debase or humble, and
may or may not be reflexive. (The committee's report *demeaned* us.)

Democrat, Democratic   In politics, it's *Democratic* for the party and references to the party (the *Democratic* platform) and *Democrat* for a member
of the *Democratic* Party. *Democrat* Party is wrong.

demolish, destroy   To say something was "completely *destroyed*" or
"completely *demolished*" is usually redundant.

denote   See CONNOTE, DENOTE.

depart   Its main prepositions are *for*, as in start, set out (*departing for*
Miami), *on*, as for date, time, or event (*departed on* vacation, will *depart on*
Friday), and *from* as for leave, diverge, deviate (*departing from* Chicago,
departing from the textbook).

depart, tr.   The *transitive* use of *depart* has received criticism, but it is presented as standard in my current dictionaries. (Flight 12 *departs* Omaha at
10 A.M. He *departed* this life too soon.)

dependent   not *dependant*.

deprecate, depreciate   To *deprecate* means to express disapproval of. (The
teacher *deprecated* my term paper.) *Depreciate* means to belittle. (They
depreciated their role in the rescue.) They sometimes get tangled up, especially in *self-* words in which *self-deprecating* has taken over from *self-
depreciating*, a use accepted by most dictionaries.

derisive, derisory   These words are used as synonyms when they mean
expressing ridicule or deserving of ridicule (*derisive* remarks, a *derisory*
showing), but *derisory* also means ridiculously small (a *derisory* offer).

derive   usually followed by *from* (*derived* satisfaction *from* success).

desert, dessert   *Desert*, a dry, barren region, is pronounced DEZ-ert. *Dessert*, the last course of a meal, is pronounced duh-ZERT, as is the verb *desert*, to abandon.

desirable, desirous   *Desirable* means worth having or wanting, pleasing, attractive, beneficial, suitable (a *desirable* apartment, a *desirable* goal). *Desirous* means desiring, having or characterized by desire, longing, wishful, hoping (*desirous* of success).

desirous   *Desirous* is followed by *of* (*desirous of* performing well) and, less often, *to* and an infinitive (*desirous to perform* well).

despair   preposition is usually *of*. (He despaired of reaching his destination.)

destined   *Destined* may be followed by *to* plus an infinitive (*destined to become* a star), *to* followed by a noun (*destined to* a bright *future*), used infrequently, and *for* followed by a noun (*destined for success*).

destruct, self-destruct   Both of these words have become standard in a variety of forms. *Destruct* is confined largely to rockets and missiles and is used as a noun. (Start the *destruct*.), a verb (*Destruct* the rocket.), and an adjective. (*Destruct* procedure.) *Self-destruct* is used chiefly as an adjective (*self-destruct* mechanism) and a verb. (The device will *self-destruct* in ten minutes.)

develop   See DISCOVER, DEVELOP, INVENT.

deviate, digress   To *deviate* is to turn aside from a set path, course of action, standard, or doctrine. (We *deviated* from the agreed-upon course.) To *digress* is to wander from the main topic in speech or writing. (The speaker *digressed* to illustrate the lecture with an anecdote.)

Aunt Mary often digressed.

diagnose   The problem is diagnosed, not the patient. (The doctor *diagnosed* my illness as the flu.)

dialogue   This spelling is preferred over *dialog*.

dice, die   *Dice* is plural and *die* singular. (The *die* is cast. The *dice* were hot.)

diction   Technically, *diction* refers to choice of words and manner of expression, but the extension of its meaning to embrace enunciation is accepted by dictionaries and most commentators.

dictum Both *dicta* and *dictum*s are accepted for the plural, but *dicta* is used far more often.

die   Usually people die *of*, not *from*. (He *died of* cancer.)

die   See DICE, DIE.

dietitian   This spelling is preferred to *dietician*.

different   usually superfluous in construction such as "I read three *different* versions" or "I ate in three *different* restaurants."

different from, than   *Different from* is the usual construction. (My car is *different from* yours.) *Than* is used to introduce a clause. (The mood is *different than* it was last year.)

differentiate, distinguish   To *distinguish* is to recognize characteristics that identify something. (It's easy to *distinguish* a horse from a mule.) To *differentiate* is to point out differences in detail. (Sometimes it's difficult to *differentiate* love from hate.) *Distinguish* is usually followed by the preposition *from* and *differentiate* by *from*, *between*, or *among*.

differ from, differ with   *Differ from* means to be unlike; *differ with* means to disagree, although *from* is also used in this sense. (Football *differs from* rugby. The coach *differed with* the referee.)

digress   See DEVIATE, DIGRESS.

dilemma   Most usage authorities maintain that *dilemma* involves a choice one must make between two equally undesirable alternatives and should not be used as a synonym for problem or predicament. (His wife presented him with a *dilemma*: he could take her to the opera, which he detested, or they could have dinner with her mother, whom he also detested.) Most dictionaries, however, accept the application to any difficult or perplexing problem.

diphtheria   often misspelled and mispronounced *diptheria.*

direct, directly   These two words are interchangeable as adverbs meaning in a direct manner, straight. (Send it *direct* [or *directly*] to Chicago.) *Directly* alone is used for precisely, exactly (*directly* on target) or without delay, immediately. (Let me know when you are ready and I'll be there *directly.*) *Directly* also means shortly, in a little while. (They'll show up *directly.*)

disability   See INABILITY, DISABILITY.

disagree   Its preposition is usually *with.* (My proposal *disagrees with* yours. Tomatoes *disagree with* me.)

disapprove, disprove   To *disapprove* is to have an unfavorable opinion of something or to refuse approval of it. (He *disapproved* my request for expenses.) When you *disprove* something you prove it wrong. (I *disproved* their assertion.) *Disapprove* takes the preposition *of.* (They *disapproved of* their daughter's new boyfriend.)

disassemble, dissemble   To *disassemble* means to take apart. (They *disassembled* my carburetor.) To *dissemble* is to put on a false appearance to conceal your thoughts or your true feelings, to feign. (I *dissembled* my jitters with a smile.)

disassociate, dissociate   Neither is incorrect but *dissociate* is the preferred version by far.

disbar   See DEBAR, DISBAR.

disbelief, unbelief   *Disbelief* is the refusal or inability to believe or accept something as true. *Unbelief* is lack of belief, skepticism, suspicion, incredulity, especially in religious matters.

disburse, disperse   *Disburse* means to pay out, expend. (The will spelled out how the funds from the estate would be *disbursed.*) *Disperse* means to scatter. (The police *dispersed* the angry crowd.)

disc, disk   These two words are interchangeable, but generally *disc* is preferred for audio and video recordings (*disc* jockey, compact *disc*) and *disk* for other uses (*disk* harrow, slipped *disk*, floppy *disk*).

disclose, divulge   Both words mean to impart information previously kept secret. *Divulge* implies a breach of confidence that *disclose* does not (*divulged* the theft charges that had been brought ten years before, *disclosed* the itinerary).

discomfit, discomfort   In strict usage, *discomfit* means to thwart, frustrate, utterly defeat. (A surprise move *discomfited* the chess player.) It has become standard for *discomfort* to mean, when used in the sense of to distress, to disconcert or to make uncomfortable (*discomfited* by the question).

discover, develop, invent   To *discover* is to gain knowledge of or find or learn about something already in existence (*discovered* America). To *develop* is to improve, advance, or perfect something that already exists (*developed* strong muscles). To *invent* is to devise, create (*invented* the can opener).

discreet, discrete   *Discreet* is prudent, circumspect, careful (*discreet* in their handling of the situation). *Discrete* is separate, distinct, detached. (The legislative, judicial, and executive branches are *discrete* parts of the U.S. government.)

disfranchise, disenfranchise   *Disenfranchise* is not incorrect, but the preference is *disfranchise*.

disinterested, uninterested   A *disinterested* person is impartial, unbiased, without personal interest in a matter. (A *disinterested* party was asked to decide the dispute.) An *uninterested* person is bored, indifferent, or lacking interest. (The visitor was *uninterested* in the antics of the children.) *Disinterested* is often used in the sense of *indifferent*. This use is rejected by most commentators and a couple of dictionaries. Some dictionaries accept it but offer a word of caution. *Uninterested* is seldom used in the *impartial* sense.

disk   See DISC, DISK.

disparage   See BELITTLE, DISPARAGE.

disparate   Its primary meaning is distinct, dissimilar, different. (Their *disparate* backgrounds led to conflict. The *disparate* group sought common ground.) Less often, it is used for *unequal* (*disparate* treatment), which is not accepted by many dictionaries.

disperse See DISBURSE, DISPERSE.

displace, misplace To *displace* is to move something from its proper place (*displaced* person, residents *displaced* by rising water). To *misplace* is to put in a wrong place, to lose or mislay. (I *misplaced* my glasses.)

disposal, disposition There are distinctions between these words. *Disposal* usually involves getting rid of—destruction, throwing away, giving away (*disposal* of unused items); *disposition* deals with administering, arranging, settling, taking care of, usually in accordance with a preconceived plan (*disposition* of troops, *disposition* of a court suit). There are occasional instances of overlap between the words, which is allowed by recent dictionaries.

disprove See DISAPPROVE, DISPROVE.

disqualify followed by *from* or *for*. (Her job *disqualified* her *from* entering the contest. His criminal record *disqualified* him *for* the position. He was *disqualified for* improper conduct.)

disregard uses prepositions *for* and *of* (showed *disregard for* their safety, displayed a *disregard of* the needs of other departments).

dissemble See DISASSEMBLE, DISSEMBLE.

dissent Its preposition is *from* (*dissented from* the majority opinion).

dissociate See DISASSOCIATE, DISSOCIATE.

distinct, distinctive, distinguished *Distinct* is unmistakable, easily perceived, separate (a *distinct* improvement). *Distinctive* is distinguished from others, characteristic, typical (*distinctive* markings). *Distinguished* is eminent, renowned, outstanding (the *distinguished* scholar).

distinguish See DIFFERENTIATE, DISTINGUISH.

distinguished See DISTINCT, DISTINCTIVE, DISTINGUISHED.

dived, dove Both are standard as the past tense of *dive*. (They *dived* off the cliff. We *dove* into the pool.) The predominant past participle is *dived*. (I have *dived* into this lake many times.)

divest   This word takes the preposition *of* and is often used reflexively. (The company *divested* itself *of* several holdings. I *divested* myself *of* my coat. We *divested* them *of* their authority.)

divulge   See DISCLOSE, DIVULGE.

doctorate, doctoral   A *doctorate* is the degree of doctor, the highest conferred by a university (a *doctorate* in physics). *Doctoral* means pertaining to or characteristic of a doctor or doctorate. (They completed their *doctoral* requirements.)

domicile   house or home. There's a temptation to spell it *domecile* or, sometimes, *domocile*.

donut   This shortened version of *doughnut* should be avoided in serious writing.

dote   uses the preposition *on*. (They *dote on* their grandchildren.)

dove   See DIVED, DOVE.

downward, downwards   *Downward* is preferred, although *downwards* is accepted, mostly as an adverb. Only *downward* is used as an attributive adjective, as in "a *downward* glance."

draft, draught   *Draft* is the primary form for all uses in American English. In Britain, *draught* is preferred for a number of meanings.

dreamed, dreamt   Both are acceptable as the past tense and past participle of *dream*. Both use the preposition *of* or *about*. (I *dreamt of* riches. I *dreamed about* the upcoming test.)

drench   Followed by prepositions *in, with*, and *by*. (The fruitcake was *drenched in* whisky. The burning kitchen was *drenched with* foam. I was *drenched by* water splashed by a passing car.)

drought, drouth   Both are standard English, but *drought* is preferred. (The storm ended a three-month *drought*.)

drowned   He or she *drowned* is the proper term. (She *drowned* in the canal.) To say someone *was drowned* might imply foul play. (He *was drowned* by two thugs who attacked him on the bridge. Wrong: He *was drowned* while swimming with friends.)

drunk, drunken   The past tense is *drank*, past participle *drunk*. *Drunken* is usually used as an attributive adjective (*drunken* driver) and *drunk* in the predicate. (The driver was drunk.)

dry   When applied to prohibitionists, the plural is *drys*.

due to, because   *Due to* may modify a noun. (My hesitation was *due to* fear.) Most dictionaries and commentators discourage its use to modify a verb. (I hesitated *due to* fear.) The second example could read, "I hesitated because of fear."

duffel   *Duffle* is not incorrect for the coarse cloth, but *duffel* is the preferred spelling (*duffel* bag).

dumb   This word is widely used colloquially for *stupid*, but this usage is not recommended for formal speech or writing.

dumbfound, dumfound   *Dumbfound* is the preferred spelling, though both forms are allowed.

dwarf   *Dwarfs* and *dwarves* are both acceptable for the plural, but *dwarfs* is more common.

dwell   Its past tense and past participle are *dwelt* and *dwelled*, with *dwelt* preferred (*dwelt* in the woods, *dwelled* on the past).

dyeing, dying   *Dyeing* and *dying* are sometimes confused. *Dyeing* comes from *dye* and *dying* from *die*.

dysfunction   Not *disfunction*. This word means impaired or abnormal functioning, as of an organ or body part or, sometimes, a family or some other social unit (*dysfunctional* liver, *dysfunctional* family).

E

each takes the singular construction. (*Each* child has an opportunity. *Each* has an opportunity), except when it follows a plural noun or pronoun. (The children *each* have an opportunity.)

each and every This phrase is redundant, but if you use it, make it singular. (*Each and every* dog has a bone to pick.)

each other, one another These two phrases are interchangeable whether they refer to two persons or things or more than two. Possessives are *each other's* and *one another's*. If you wish to make a distinction, use *each other* for two and *one another* for more than two. (The two partners hated *each other*. The three partners hated *one another*.)

eager Its most common preposition is *to* with the infinitive (*eager to* start). It is also used with *for* (*eager for* results) and *in* (*eager in* their search for knowledge). See ANXIOUS, EAGER.

earthly, earthy *Earthly* means of or pertaining to earth, as opposed to heaven (an *earthly* paradise), or possible or conceivable. (I have no *earthly* use for that.) *Earthy* means resembling or consisting of earth or soil (an *earthy* mixture) or realistic, coarse, crude, or unrefined. (She uses *earthy* language.)

easy, easily *Easy* is an adjective and *easily* is an adverb. (They wanted *easy* jobs. Our team won *easily*.) *Easy* appears as an adverb only in colloquialisms (*easy* come, *easy* go, go *easy* on, *easy* does it, take it *easy*, and rest *easy*.)

eclectic selected from various systems, doctrines, methods, ideas, tastes, or styles (an *eclectic* set of principles). The key here is diversity, not quality.

ecology, environment *Ecology* applies to relations between organisms and their environment, and *environment* applies to external factors that influence the development of organisms—climate, soil, minerals, etc. The two terms should not be used synonymously.

economic, economical   As a rule, you use *economical* when you mean money-saving or efficient use of wealth and resources (an *economical* household budget) and *economic* when you are referring to the production, distribution, and use of income, wealth, and commodities, or the science of economics (*economic* aid for the Third World).

ecstasy   sometimes misspelled *ecstacy.*

effect   See AFFECT, EFFECT.

effete   sterile, unable to produce, spent, exhausted, worn out (the *effete* leadership on the aging English staff). It also means decadent, overrefined, soft, weak, degenerate—a newer sense accepted by dictionaries. (The club was too *effete* for old-fashioned folks like us.)

e.g., i.e   Both terms are abbreviations for Latin phrases; *e.g.* stands for *exempli gratia*—for example (the leading economic indexes, *e.g.*, Dow-Jones), and *i.e.* for *id est*—that is (the majority of the bookstore's customers, *i.e.*, students). They are sometimes confused.

egoist, egotist   An *egoist* espouses a doctrine that self-interest is the foundation of morality. An *egotist* is one who refers to himself or herself excessively, a conceited person, a braggart with an inflated opinion of his or her worth or importance. Sometimes *egoist* is used for *egotist*, but this is not encouraged by most commentators and dictionaries.

egregious   This word once meant distinguished, eminent, remarkable. It now means the reverse—remarkably bad, outstanding for undesirable qualities, flagrant (the *egregious* wrongs inflicted on my client). The earlier meanings, when they appear, are labeled archaic.

either   As an adjective or pronoun it means one or the other of two. The pronoun takes a singular verb. (*Either* is appropriate. Take *either* horse.)

either/or, neither/nor   When these conjunctions connect singular subjects, a singular verb is required. (*Neither* Jack *nor* Ethel was at home.) When one of the subjects is plural and the other singular, the verb takes the number of the nearest noun or pronoun. (*Either* the teacher *or* the parents are wrong. *Either* the parents *or* the teacher is wrong.)

eke out   to add to, supplement with great effort. (I *eked out* my income with a night job.) It also means to earn laboriously, with great difficulty (*eked out* a living).

elder, older   Use *elder* and *eldest* for people, *older* and *oldest* for things and people. (My car's *older* than yours.) *Elder* and *eldest* mainly indicate relative age of the members of a family (*elder* brother, the *eldest* child) and seniority, in which case *elder* may not necessarily be *older* (*elder* partner, *elder* statesman).

elegy, eulogy   An *elegy* is a song or poem of lament for the dead ("Elegy Written in a Country Churchyard"). *A eulogy* is a spoken or written statement of praise, especially for someone who has died. (A brother delivered the *eulogy* at the funeral.)

"Elemental, dear Watson."

elemental, elementary   A number of usage guides would restrict *elemental's* primary meaning to the forces of nature and the elements earth, wind, air, and fire, literally (the *elemental* fury of the hurricane) and figuratively (their *elemental* anger that destroyed the project), and *elementary's* to simple, basic, introductory (an *elementary* guide to physics). Some recent desk dictionaries permit interchangeable uses.

elicit, illicit   *Elicit* means to draw forth (elicit a response), and *illicit* means unlawful (an *illicit* operation).

eligible   Its usual prepositions are *for* followed by a noun (*eligible for* a parole) and *to* followed by an infinitive (*eligible to* participate).

else   When *else* follows a pronoun, the possessive is formed by adding apostrophe *s* to *else* (someone *else's*, everyone *else's*). The possessive with *who* can be either "who else's" or "whose else."

emanate   *Emanate's* preposition is *from* (an odor *emanating from* the ditch).

embark   uses the preposition *on* or *upon* for an activity (*embarked on* a new project, *embarked upon* a journey), *for* for destination (*embarked for* Chicago), and *from* for point of departure (*embarked from* New York).

endemic, epidemic, pandemic **49**

embarrass   Double *r*, double *s*.

embellish   Its most common preposition is *with* (*embellished* the speech *with* some funny examples), although *by* is sometimes found.

emend   See AMEND, EMEND.

emigrate, immigrate, migrate   To *emigrate* is to leave a country to settle in another. To *immigrate* is to move to a country to take up residence. People emigrate *from* and immigrate *to*. *Migrate* simply means to travel from one place to another and applies to either people or animals.

eminent, imminent   *Eminent* means distinguished, outstanding, high in rank, noteworthy, prominent (an *eminent* diplomat, *eminently* fair). *Imminent* means likely to occur at any moment. (The invasion was *imminent*.)

emote   To express emotion in acting or as if acting, usually in an exaggerated or theatrical manner. Some authorities and dictionaries label it colloquial.

empathy, sympathy   *Empathy* is identification with and understanding of another's situation, feelings, and motives. (The negotiator, once a prisoner of war, *empathized* with the hostages.) *Sympathy* is harmony of or agreement in feeling, compassion, commiseration. (We *sympathized* with the couple whose car broke down.)

emporium   Its plurals are *emporiums* and *emporia*. *Emporiums* is more common.

enamor   to fill with love, to charm, captivate. It usually appears passively with the preposition *of* (*enamored of* the new employee).

ended, ending   *Ended* is usually used for what has come to an end and *ending* for what is coming to an end. (The report reviewed the year *ended* June 30. The work will be done in the six months *ending* in April.) *Ending* may also be used for a past action. (They took part in the program *ending* last June.)

endemic, epidemic, pandemic   *Endemic* applies to something, often a disease, prevalent in or peculiar to a particular region or group of people (a disease *endemic* to the southeastern United States, an attitude *endemic* to sports writers). An *epidemic* is the rapid spread of a disease through a community (an *epidemic* of scarlet fever). *Pandemic* refers to a disease that is universal or general, prevalent over a wide area, such as a country, continent, or the world.

end result   *End* can often be eliminated.

enervate   To *enervate* means to deprive of strength, force, vigor, to weaken. (The heat wave *enervated* the workers.) It is often used erroneously as a synonym for invigorate or energize.

Englishman   See BRITON, BRITISHER, ENGLISHMAN.

enhance   This verb almost always has a thing, rather than a person, as its object. (A coat of paint *enhances* the value of the house. A cheerful manner and careful dress will *enhance* your career.)

enormity, enormousness   *Enormity* means great wickedness. (The *enormity* of his crimes shocked the nation.) *Enormousness* means great size, vastness, or immensity (the *enormousness* of the task, the *enormousness* of the building). Although a great number of people use *enormity* in reference to great size, most usage commentators recommend preserving the distinction between *enormity* and *enormousness*, and most recent dictionaries caution that the use of *enormity* in the sense of immensity is considered nonstandard by many people. If you use it, make sure the meaning is clear. Avoid phrases like "the enormity of their business dealings."

enquire   See INQUIRE, ENQUIRE.

en route   Two words are preferred.

ensure, insure   Both terms are used for "make certain," with *ensure* preferred. (The additional capital *ensured* our success.) Only *insure* is used in the commercial sense. (Our policy *insured* us against wind and flood damage.)

enthuse   colloquial expression for "to show enthusiasm" or "to fill with enthusiasm."

entomology, etymology   *Entomology* is the study of insects. *Etymology* is the study of the origin and development of words.

envelop, envelope   To *envelop* is to enclose, to surround entirely. (The flames *enveloped* the house.) An *envelope* is a thin paper container for a letter or the like. (The check came in a brown *envelope*.)

enviable, envious   *Enviable* means extremely desirable. (The agreement left them in an *enviable* position.) *Envious* means full of envy, feeling envy. (We were *envious* of their position.)

environment   See ECOLOGY, ENVIRONMENT.

epidemic   See ENDEMIC, EPIDEMIC, PANDEMIC.

epitaph, epigraph   An *epigraph* is an inscription on a building or statue. It is also a quotation at the beginning of a book or a chapter of a book to suggest its theme. An *epitaph* is an inscription on a tomb or gravestone in memory of the person buried there. It is also a brief statement paying tribute to a deceased person.

epithet   a descriptive word or phrase, often abusive, added to or used instead of a name (Eric the Red, Alexander the Great, Ivan the Terrible, America the Beautiful, Doctor Death, Queen of Mean, Tricky Dick, Slick Willy, dirty rat, rotten liar, yellow-bellied coward, egghead, angel of mercy).

Slick Willy   Tricky Dick   Honest Abe

epitome   This does not mean acme, the best, high point, or climax. It is a brief summary of a book, report, incident, etc., an abstract. It is also an ideal representative or example of a class or type, embodiment (the *epitome* of kindness, the *epitome* of mediocrity).

equable, equitable   *Equable* means free from variations, uniform, steady, not easily disturbed (a climate characterized by *equable* temperatures, well liked for a good nature and *equable* temper). *Equitable* is fair and just (an *equitable* agreement).

equal   This does not usually need comparative forms such as *most equal* or *more equal*.

equal to   *Equal* is most often used with *to* and, infrequently, *with* (*equal to* the task, *equal to* handling the situation).

equally as   This term is usually redundant. Use *as* when a comparison occurs within the sentence and *equally* when the comparison is implied. (Our position was *as* firm as it was at the beginning. Our position was *equally* firm.)

equitable   See EQUABLE, EQUITABLE.

equivalent   The adjective takes the preposition *to*. (The statement was *equivalent to* a concession.) The noun takes *of*. (The statement was the *equivalent of* a concession.)

equivocal   See AMBIGUOUS, EQUIVOCAL.

errata   This is the plural of *erratum*, which means a mistake in printing or writing. (The *errata* are found in three chapters.) *Errata* is also a list correcting such errors, usually inserted in a book after it is printed, and in this sense it is sometimes used as singular. The singular form for the list is criticized by most usage guides. (The *errata* are in Appendix A.)

escape   This verb requires *from* when used as an intransitive verb meaning to get out of a place of confinement. (They *escaped* from prison. Gas *escaped* from the ruptured pipe.) The preposition is not needed when the verb is transitive meaning avoid, evade, elude. (They *escaped* notice. Nothing *escapes* them.)

escapee   Current dictionaries consider *escapee* a respectable word for a person who has *escaped* from confinement. It is opposed by some usage authorities, including a handful who prefer *escaper*.

especial, special   Both are acceptable as adjectives, although *special* is far more widely used, but a strict distinction exists between their adverbial forms. *Especially* is used in the sense of particularly or to a marked degree. (We must all be discreet, *especially* you. They are *especially* qualified.) *Specially* is used when the meaning is specifically (*specially* trained, *specially* prepared).

essay   See ASSAY, ESSAY.

essential   The adjective's primary preposition is *to*. (Salt is *essential* to the recipe.) The noun's is *of* (one of the *essentials of* life in the city). Sometimes the adjective is followed by *in*. (Discipline is *essential in* military life.)

essentially, substantially   These two words are interchangeable in the sense of *basically*. (The reports were *essentially* [or *substantially*] the same.) But they do perform different functions as adjectives. An *essential* contribution is one that is indispensable, one that means the difference between success and failure. A *substantial* contribution is one that is considerable but not indispensable.

estimate   The verb *estimate* most often uses the preposition *at*. (The crowd was *estimated at* 45,000.) The noun usually takes *of*. (What is your *estimate of* their worth?)

estrange   used with the preposition *from* (*estranged from* the fans who once adored them, *estranged from* his wife.)

et al.   abbreviation for a Latin term, *et alii* or *et alia*. It means "and others." It is used with a period (*et al.*) or without, and in italic type (*et al.*) or roman (et al.). Current desk dictionaries prefer the period and roman. (Mary Jones, John Smith et al. presented the opponents' side.)

etc.   abbreviation for *et cetera*. It means *and others of the same kind, and so forth*. *And et cetera* is redundant.

etymology   See ENTOMOLOGY, ETYMOLOGY.

eulogy   See ELEGY, EULOGY.

even-steven   This is the preferred construction; also *even-stephen*. Colloquial. It means share and share alike, having no balance and no debt on either side, or tied score. (We were *even-steven* after four sets.)

everybody, everyone   These words require singular verbs and pronouns. (*Everyone* has his [or her] book.) If this results in an awkward or politically offensive construction, recast the sentence. See ANYBODY, ANYONE.

every day, everyday   This adverbial phrase that means each day is two words. (We go there *every day*.) The adjective meaning daily, ordinary, commonplace is one word (an *everyday* occurrence, *everyday* shoes).

everyone, every one   The pronoun is one word. (*Everyone* was there.) As two words, *every one* means each one and is followed by *of*. (*Every one* of the students failed.)

every other   every second, every alternate. (Payday is *every other* Friday. We had a meeting *every other* day.)

evident   See APPARENT, EVIDENT.

exceedingly, excessively   *Exceedingly* means to an unusual degree, very, extremely. *Excessively* means going beyond what is usual, proper, reasonable, or necessary. (The sales representative was *exceedingly* nice. The room was *excessively* hot.)

except   takes an objective pronoun when used as a preposition meaning but, other than, excluding. (Everyone was there *except* me.) See ACCEPT, EXCEPT.

exception   Its prepositions are *to* and *of* (an *exception to* the rule, made an *exception of* the rigid policy) and its chief idioms are *take exception to* and *with the exception of*. (I *took exception to* their remarks. They all missed four meetings *with* the *exception of* the president.)

exceptionable, exceptional   *Exceptional* means out of the ordinary, unusual, uncommon (an *exceptional* child who reads at the age of four). *Exceptionable* means objectionable, open to exception. (We considered our guest's behavior *exceptionable*.)

excessively   See EXCEEDINGLY, EXCESSIVELY.

exclude   uses the preposition *from* (*excluded from* the meeting).

exclusive   most often followed by the preposition *of*. (The price was $200,000, *exclusive of* the agent's commission.) It sometimes uses *to* (a belief not *exclusive to* Christians).

excuse   followed by prepositions *from* and *for* (*excused from* jury duty, *excused for* being late). See APOLOGY, EXCUSE.

exemplary   primary meaning *worthy of imitation*, a sense that should be present when *exemplary* is used to describe *excellence* (*exemplary* behavior, *exemplary* conduct).

exhausting, exhaustive   *Exhausting* is using up, consuming, draining (an *exhausting* trip). *Exhaustive* is comprehensive, thorough (*exhaustive* detail).

exhilarate   not *exhilirate* or *exhilerate*.

existence   sometimes misspelled *existance*.

exonerate   Its prepositions are *from* and *of* (*exonerated from* suspicion of theft, *exonerated of* conspiracy).

exorbitant   not *exhorbitant*.

exorcise   *exorcise* preferred to *exorcize*. It is sometimes confused with *exercise*.

expatriate   commonly misspelled *expatriot*. It's a person who takes up residence in another country or who renounces allegiance to his or her native land.

expect   often followed by *to* and infinitive. (I *expect to be* in Pittsburgh by sundown.), *from* (they explained what they *expected from* us), and *of*. (They *expected* more *of* us.)

expect, suppose   The use of *expect* in the sense of to presume, to suppose, to guess, to think is colloquial. (I *expect* they'll be hungry when they get here.)

expel   Its preposition is *from* (*expelled from* college).

experienced   usually followed by the preposition *in* (*experienced in* construction work).

extemporaneous, impromptu   *Extemporaneous* refers to a speech given from an outline or notes rather than text or memory. (She spoke *extemporaneously* from notes prepared on the way to the meeting.) *Impromptu* describes a speech given on the spur of the moment, unexpectedly, with no preparation. (The surprise guest offered a few *impromptu* remarks.)

extended, extensive   *Extended* is stretched or pulled out, prolonged (an *extended* visit, *extended* remarks). *Extensive* is vast, broad, wide (*extensive* knowledge, *extensive* land holdings).

extract   Its main preposition is *from*. (The team *extracted* a great amount of satisfaction *from* its victory.)

exuberant   sometimes misspelled *exhuberant*.

They were exuberant when they heard the news.

F

facetious   frequently misspelled.

face up to   an acceptable idiom meaning to confront with courage (*faced up to* a difficult situation).

fact that   Often, *the fact that* can be replaced by *that*. (The mayor acknowledged *the fact that* [*that*] the aide provided misinformation.) However, it comes in handy to introduce a noun clause (The board ignored *the fact that* the company's stock had fallen.) or after a preposition. (They referred to *the fact that* the team was undefeated.)

factor   *Factor* is properly used as an element that contributes to a result. (Allegations of misconduct were a *factor in* the incumbent's defeat.) "Contributing *factor*" is redundant.

fail   *To fail* applies to an unmet objective, obligation, intention, or expectation. (The team *failed* to reach the finals. They *failed* to appear. The guard *failed* to challenge the intruder.) Do not use it in other senses merely to express a negative. (I *failed to* think of it.)

famed, famous   *Famed* is accepted as a synonym for *famous* but it is more commonly used in the predicate, usually followed by *for*. (The city was *famed for* its cathedrals.) *Famous* is used both as an attributive (a *famous* speaker) and in the predicate (*famous for* his talent with the trombone).

familiar   usually used with the preposition *with* (*familiar with* the operation) and sometimes *to*. (His name was *familiar to* them.)

farther, further   Restrict *farther* to physical distance and use *further* for distance and other senses, such as moreover, more extended, and additional. (They traveled eight miles *farther*. *Further*, he plans to sue us. No *further* discussion was necessary.)

fascinate   used with *by* when the object is a person or a thing (*fascinated by* the speaker, *fascinated by* their wealth). When *fascinate* is followed by *with*, the object is usually inanimate (*fascinated with* the proposal).

fascination   Its main prepositions are *for, with*, and *of.* Make it clear who or what the object of fascination is (the *fascination of* the hunt, our *fascination for* adventure, their *fascination with* the puzzle).

fatal, fateful   Although these two words tend to overlap, a number of commentators and some dictionaries would preserve a distinction: use of *fatal* to mean "causing death or capable of resulting in destruction, disaster, or ruin" and use of *fateful* to mean "having important consequences." (The plant's closing was a *fatal* blow to the town. The move to close the plant was a *fateful* decision.)

father-in-law   plural *fathers-in-law.*

fault   *fault* acceptable as a verb meaning "to criticize" or "to find fault with." (I can't *fault* his presentation.)

favorable   followed by the prepositions *to* (a position *favorable to* our side, weather *favorable to* gardeners), and *for* (a climate *favorable for* growing cotton).

faze, phase   The spelling of the verb *faze* is preferred to the rarely seen *feaze* and *feeze*. It means to disturb, daunt, or disconcert, and ordinarily is used with a negative. (Nothing *fazed* them. They were not *fazed*.) *Phase* is a noun that means aspect or stage. It is sometimes used incorrectly for *faze*, but *faze* is seldom used for *phase*.

feasible, possible   *Possible* means there is a likelihood something can be done and *feasible* means not only can it be done, but it is desirable to do it. (Studies show that it is *possible* to build a tunnel through the mountain. The report concludes that building a tunnel through the mountain is *feasible*.) *Possible* also can refer to the likelihood of something happening. (Severe weather is *possible* tonight.) *Feasible* cannot work in this sense.

feed   most often followed by *on* or *upon*. (Their discontent *feeds on* their coworkers' complaints.) and sometimes *off* (They *feed off* the land.) and *into*. (The river *feeds into* the sea.)

ferment, foment   These words are to a certain extent interchangeable. *Ferment* means to excite, stir up, cause to seethe with excitement or agitation, *foment* to stimulate, encourage, foster, promote the growth or spread of. It nearly always has a bad meaning—foment unrest, rebellion, sedition, trouble, discontent. *Ferment* has the broader range of meanings—good and bad (ideas *fermenting* in the research department, new plot *fermenting* in the rebels' camp).

fetch   to go after something and come back with it. (She went to the store to *fetch* bread and milk.) It also means to bring a price, as at an auction. (The lamp *fetched* $500 at the estate sale.)

fewer, less   Use *less* for quantity and abstractions (*less* sugar, *less* integrity) and *fewer* for countable things (*fewer* ships, *fewer* people). *Less than* is used before plural nouns that indicate amount, time, and distance (*less* than 60 miles, *less* than 40 years, *less* than 60 pounds).

fiancé, fiancée   respectively, a man and a woman who are engaged to be married.

fiddle, violin   The instrument is called a *fiddle* when used in country music. *Fiddle* is considered informal, sometimes even derogatory, in more formal contexts, where *violin* is the proper term.

fight with   *Fight with* can be ambiguous. For example, "He *fought with* the rebels" could raise the question of which side. *Fought against* could clear this up if the rebels were the enemy. Usually, though, the context makes the meaning clear.

figuratively   See LITERALLY, FIGURATIVELY.

figure   informal when used as a verb meaning conclude, judge, or believe.

figurehead   a person who is head of something in title only, having no real authority or responsibility. (The president was a *figurehead* who was manipulated by the junta.)

final, finale   *Final* as an adjective means coming at the end, last in place, order or time (the *final* chapter) and as a noun, usually plural, it refers to the last of a series of athletic contests (the state basketball *finals*) or the last and decisive test in an academic course. (We passed our *finals*.) *Finale*, a noun, means the concluding part of something, usually a musical composition or program or the concluding part of a proceedings. (The concert's *finale* was a work by Beethoven.)

finalize   Although it is frequently used as a verb meaning to conclude, to complete, to finish, to put into final form, it is not recommended for serious speech or writing. (They *finalized* the report.)

firefighter, fireman   The term *firefighter* more precisely fits the occupation than *fireman*, which is better suited for a person who stokes furnaces on trains, ships, etc. *Firefighter* also is preferred by the men and women who fight the fires.

first, firstly   both acceptable for introducing a series: "first, secondly, thirdly," "firstly, secondly, thirdly," or, perhaps the simplest construction, "first, second, third."

firsthand   One word is recommended: *"firsthand* knowledge."

first two   this construction preferred to *two first*, although *two first* is not incorrect. (I read the *first two* books of the trilogy.)

fish, fishes   both terms allowed as the plural, with *fish* used collectively. (We caught a lot of *fish*), and *fishes* used when more than one kind is involved. (The *fishes* found there include tarpon and sailfish.)

fit, fitted   either form permissible for the past tense and past participle of *fit*, although *fitted* is preferred when the meaning is "to adjust, make conform, to cause to *fit*." (I was *fitted* for a suit. The suit *fit* well the last time I wore it.)

flagrant   See BLATANT, FLAGRANT.

flak, flack   *Flak* is antiaircraft fire and, figuratively, criticism or opposition, a use considered informal or colloquial by some dictionaries. (The proposal received a lot of *flak*.) *Flack* is slang for a press agent or publicist. (The senator's *flack* bought a round of drinks.) Some dictionaries give *flack* as a variant of *flak*.

flammable, inflammable   both acceptable for combustible. *Inflammable* is widely used, though *flammable* is preferred by scientists and technical writers, as well as safety authorities who fear that people may mistake *inflammable* for "not combustible."

flaunt, flout   To *flaunt* is to display ostentatiously or defiantly (*flaunted* their jewelry). To *flout* is to show scorn or contempt for (*flouted* the traffic laws).

flautist, flutist   *Flutist* is preferred.

flied   In baseball, the past tense and past participle of *fly*—to hit a *fly* ball—is *flied*, not *flew* or *flown*. You can say "The batter *flied* to left field," but you shouldn't say "The bird *flied* to the top of the tree."

flier, flyer   *Flier* is the choice in nearly all uses—aviator, handbill, etc.—though *flyer* appears in the names of some trains and buses.

flounder, founder   *Flounder* means to thrash about, to struggle clumsily (*flounder* in the mud), to proceed in confusion (*flounder* for an explanation). *Founder* means to fill with water and sink (The ship *foundered* in heavy seas.) or to fail, collapse (The troubled company finally *foundered*.).

flout   See FLAUNT, FLOUT.

fluorescent   sometimes misspelled *flourescent*.

flutist   See FLAUTIST, FLUTIST.

flyer   See FLIER, FLYER.

-fold   multiplied by a specified number (a *fivefold* increase) or having a specified number of parts (a *twofold* solution).

following   frowned on by some usage guides as a preposition used in place of *after*. (*Following* the speech, we took questions from the floor.)

She had a fondness for birds.

foment   See FERMENT, FOMENT.

fond, fondness   *Fond* is followed by the preposition *of* (*fond of* chocolate). *Fondness* uses the preposition *for* (a *fondness for* animals).

forbear, forebear   *Forbear*, a verb, means to refrain from, resist, hold back, to control oneself under provocation (to *forbear* responding to the insult). *Forebear*, a noun, means ancestor. (My *forebears* came from England.)

forbid   Followed by an infinitive (Mom *forbids* me to date.), a gerund (The company *forbids* smoking.), or a noun (Traffic laws *forbid* U-turns.). Avoid *from*. (The company *forbids* its employees *from* smoking.) The past tense is *forbade*, sometimes *forbad*, and its past participle is usually *forbidden*.

forcible, forceful *Forcible* is most commonly used in physical contexts (*forcible* entry, *forcible* ejection) and *forceful* in figurative contexts (a *forceful* speaker, a *forceful* personality).

forecasted not incorrect, but *forecast* is favored as past tense and past participle of *forecast*.

forego, forgo To *forego* is to go before, precede (a *foregone* conclusion, the *foregoing* text). To *forgo* means to abstain or refrain from, to do without. (I will *forgo* dessert.)

foreword a brief introduction to a published work, usually a book and usually written by someone other than the book's author. It sometimes appears incorrectly as *forward* or *foreward*.

former, latter *Former* is used to refer to the first of two persons or things, and *latter* is used to refer to the second. Neither should be used when three or more persons or things are involved. (Smith and Jones ran neck and neck most of the night, but the *former* prevailed. Wrong: White, Jones, and Smith ran neck and neck most of the night but the *latter* prevailed.)

formulas, formulae either form acceptable as the plural of *formula*. *Formulas* is more common.

fortuitous, fortunate *Fortuitous* means happening by chance, accidental; *fortunate* refers to something resulting from good luck, good fortune. A *fortunate* encounter is one that proves beneficial; a *fortuitous* encounter may prove *fortunate* but it may also have unhappy results. (A note found on the victim described a *fortuitous* meeting [by chance] two months before with the person accused of killing him.)

forward, forwards *Forward* preferred, especially before a noun (a *forward* motion, a *forward* child).

founded used with *on, upon*, and *in*—most often *on* (a novel that was *founded on* a true story).

founder See FLOUNDER, FOUNDER.

Frankenstein   *Frankenstein* was the creator, not the monster, but, *Frankenstein* has come to mean something that destroys or presents a danger to the one who originated it.

friend   Its usual preposition is *of* (a *friend of* mine, *friends of* the symphony) and sometimes *to*. (The principal is no *friend to* our children.) *Friend* is accompanied by *with* in the idioms *to be friends with* and *to make friends with*.

from, in   The U.S. fought in World War II "*in* 1941–1945 [a period of time]," not "*from* 1941–1945." But "*from* 1941 to 1945 [from one year to another]" is correct.

from...through   "*From* Monday *to* Friday" refers to a four-day period. If you want to include Friday, make it "*from* Monday *through* Friday"—up to and including Friday.

from...to   It's *from ... to* and *between ... and*: (We'll meet sometime *between* now *and* Friday. Profits increased *from* 5 percent last year *to* 8 percent this year.)

frown   usually followed by *on* or *upon*. (Gambling is *frowned on* in this club.) Sometimes *at* is used. (I *frowned at* the dealer.)

fugitive   Its preposition is *from* (a *fugitive from* the county jail).

-ful   The plural of words created by adding this suffix is formed by adding *s* to the suffix: cupfuls, teaspoonfuls, roomfuls, bucketfuls. Inserting the *s* after the stem is colloquial: bucketsful, teaspoonsful.

full   usually followed by *of* (a box *full of* presents).

fulsome   excessive, overdone to the point of disgust, offensively flattering, or insincere. In other words, the frequently used *fulsome* praise doesn't mean full or abundant. Instead, *fulsome* is used like this: "fawning and *fulsome* assistant," "gaudy and *fulsome* furnishings."

funeral, funereal   *Funeral* as an adjective is used mostly in an attributive position in the sense of pertaining to a funeral (*funeral* arrangements, *funeral* procession). *Funereal* means of or suitable for a funeral—sad, solemn, gloomy, dismal, dark. (The losers' locker room took on a *funereal* atmosphere.)

funeral director   See MORTICIAN.

further   See FARTHER, FURTHER.

G

gaiety   frequently misspelled.

gainsay   an oldie that means to declare something to be false, to deny, contradict, or oppose. (I would not *gainsay* your assertion.) *Gainsay* is not very common these days. It's viewed variously by usage writers and dictionaries as literary, old-fashioned, archaic, and formal.

gambit   Like the chess opening in which one or more pieces are sacrificed to create a strategic position, the extended use of *gambit* is to make a concession at the start of negotiations or the like to gain a later advantage. (The union negotiator offered to trim the union's salary request as talks got under way. The company has not yet responded to the *gambit*.) Often applied to any remark intended to open a conversation. This use is accepted by current dictionaries.

gamut   *Gamut*, originally applied to a series of musical notes, now most often refers figuratively to a complete range or scale, and in this sense a *gamut* is usually *run* (*ran* the *gamut* of emotions from joy to sorrow).

gantlet, gauntlet   A *gantlet* is two lines of people who beat someone forced to run between them. The word is now used figuratively to describe a severe test or ordeal. (He ran the *gantlet* of criticism from his colleagues.) A *gauntlet* is a glove. It also is used figuratively. To *throw down the gauntlet* is to issue a challenge; to *take up the gauntlet* is to accept a challenge. (He *threw down the gauntlet* to his corporate rivals.) *Gauntlet* is sometimes used in place of *gantlet* (run the *gauntlet*), a use accepted by dictionaries.

garnish, garnishee   To *garnish* is to adorn or decorate and is most often done to food. To *garnishee* is to attach money, usually wages, or property to satisfy a debt. *Garnish* is correct in this sense but rarely used. The process is called *garnishment*, and the debtor is called the *garnishee*.

gauge   sometimes misspelled *guage*.

gauntlet   See GANTLET, GAUNTLET.

genealogy Often incorrectly spelled *geneology*.

genial See CONGENIAL, GENIAL.

gibe, jibe *Gibe* means to taunt or to sneer or scoff at. (They *gibed at* the highly touted rookie when he made a mistake.) *Jibe* is a nautical term for changing directions. Colloquially, it also means "to be in accord with," as in "Their stories didn't *jibe* with mine," and is infrequently used for *gibe* in the taunting, sneering sense.

given, adj. (prone to) prone, disposed, inclined, having a tendency (usually followed by *to*) (*given to* violent outbursts, *given to* sarcasm).

given, adj. (specified) stated, fixed, or specified (on a *given* date, at a *given* time, at a *given* location).

given, n. an established fact, condition, factor, something taken for granted. (It's a *given* that she'll get the new position.)

gladiolus plurals are *gladioli, gladiolus*, and *gladioluses*. *Gladioli* is most common, and *gladioluses* the least common.

She was the most glamorous woman he'd ever seen.

glamour, glamorous These spellings are preferred.

glance, glimpse To *glance* is to take a quick look at something. (I *glanced* at the scoreboard. I sneaked a *glance* at the scoreboard.) A *glimpse* is a brief, momentary, incomplete view of something. (I caught a *glimpse* of the car as it roared by.) A *glimpse,* some usage guides say, is what is revealed by a *glance*. Usually you *take a glance* and *get* or *catch a glimpse*.

glow most often used with the preposition *with* (*glowed with* pride).

goes without saying an idiom that refers to something usually better left unsaid.

good, well *Good* is an adjective and should not be used as an adverb. Say "a good book" or "I'm in *good* health" but not "They play *good*." *Well* is an adverb. (They play *well*.) As an adjective it means in good health. (I am quite *well*.) When a copulative verb is involved, the same practices that apply to *bad* and *badly* apply to *good* and *well*. See BAD, BADLY.

good will, goodwill *goodwill* or *good will* for the noun, *goodwill* for attributive modifier (a gesture of *goodwill* [or *good will*], a *goodwill* gesture).

got, gotten usually *got* when the meaning is must, ought, and become (I've *got* to go. I've *got* a car. I *got* married.) *Got* is used for possess. (I've *got* five dollars.) *Gotten* is used for obtain. (I've *gotten* a new car.) Both forms are often used with *have*, *had*, etc. contracted. These terms are widely used in speech but should be avoided in serious writing.

gourmand, gourmet A *gourmand* is fond of good eating, often to excess—a glutton. A *gourmet* is a connoisseur of fine food and drink, an epicure.

graduate "I *graduated* from high school" and "I *was graduated* from high school" are both acceptable, with the former construction preferred. "I graduated high school" is not accepted.

graffiti *Graffiti* is the plural of the seldom-used *graffito* and usually is used with a plural verb. (Most of the *graffiti* were gang symbols.) It is often used as a mass noun with a singular verb. (*Graffiti* is a growing problem in big cities.) Usage guides and dictionaries are not yet ready to accept this use as standard.

grandiloquent often misspelled. It describes pompous or bombastic language.

grapple most frequently used with the preposition *with* (*grappled with* a problem, *grappled with* the realities of the situation).

grateful *Grateful* takes the preposition *for* when you are referring to something received and *to* when you are referring to people. (I'm *grateful for* your help. I'm *grateful to* you for helping me.)

grateful, gratified *Grateful* means thankful, appreciative of kindness (*grateful* for your help). *Gratified* is the past tense and participle of the verb *to gratify*, meaning to give pleasure to, to satisfy, to indulge (*gratified* by the refund, *gratified* at the compliment, *gratified* their desire for clothing).

gray, grey   Americans prefer *gray*; the British use *grey*. It's *greyhound* for both.

grieve   used with prepositions *for* (*grieved for* my lost love), *at* (*grieved at* the stranger's plight), or *over* (*grieved over* our friend's death).

grievous   not *grievious*.

grill, grille   A *grill* is a metal grate used to cook food over a flame. A *grille* is a grating that forms a screen, divider, or barrier as used in a window or gateway or in front of the radiator of a car; dictionaries give *grill* as an alternate spelling in these senses.

grisly, grizzly, grizzled   *Grisly* is gruesome, repugnant, horrible, ghastly, terrifying (a *grisly* sight at the scene of the ax murder). *Grizzly* and *grizzled* mean grayish and *grizzly* applies to some bears (*grizzly* bear, *grizzled* beard, *grizzled* veteran).

grope   most often followed by the preposition *for* (*groping for* an answer, *groping* in the darkness *for* the telephone).

H

had   Such constructions as "I *had* my house broken into" and "I *had* my leg broken" can be ambiguous and probably should be recast. It could leave the impression that the action was taken at the behest of the victim.

hail, hale   To *hail* is to welcome, greet, salute, acclaim, to call out or signal to in order to get the attention of (to *hail* a friend, to *hail* a waiter, to *hail* the new president). To *hale* is to haul, drag, compel to go (*haled* into court).

hairbreadth, hairsbreadth   Both are correct, though *hairbreadth* is a slight favorite. *Hair's breadth* is also found occasionally.

half-mast, half-staff   *Half-mast* is more common, but *half-staff* is acceptable. Some authorities insist that as a symbol of mourning, naval flags are lowered to *half-mast* and others to *half-staff*, but this distinction is not observed by current desk dictionaries.

Halloween   This construction is preferred to *Hallowe'en* for the night of celebration on the eve of All Saints' Day.

hamstring   As a verb, *hamstring* means to make ineffective or powerless. *Hamstrung* is the overwhelming choice over *hamstringed* for the past tense and past participle. (The zoning decision *hamstrung* the expansion strategy.)

hand down, hand up   A grand jury *hands up* an indictment. A judge *hands down* a decision.

hangar, hanger   A *hangar* is a building used for storing and repairing aircraft. A *hanger* is a device used for hanging things (as a coat *hanger*) or someone who hangs something (as a *paperhanger*).

hanged, hung   When executions are involved, *hanged* is the term preferred as the past tense and past participle; *hung* is the choice in all other senses. (The posse *hanged* the suspect. The suspect was *hanged*. Mom *hung* the picture.)

hara-kiri   the proper form for the ritual suicide by cutting the belly open formerly practiced by the Japanese samurai in lieu of execution or to avoid dishonor. It's from the Japanese *hara*, belly, and *kiri*, cutting. Pronounced hah-rah-KEAR-ee.

harass   often misspelled *harrass*.

harbor   See PORT, HARBOR.

hard, hardly   The use of *hardly* when you mean *severely* or *harshly* often causes confusion with the word's sense of scarcely or barely. "The company was *hardly* hit by the recession" could mean that the company was either really belted or barely touched. The adverbial form of *hard* runs no such risk. (The company was *hard* hit by the recession.) In fact, *hard* is recommended over *hardly* in any situation in which it works.

hardly   Do not use with negatives in constructions such as "I can't *hardly* believe it." or "He left without hardly a word." Make it (I can *hardly* believe it.) or (He left *without* a word.) or (He left *with hardly* a word.). *Hardly* is used with *when* instead of *than*. (We had *hardly* arrived *when* the rain started. Wrong: We had *hardly* arrived *than* the rain started.) The same applies to *scarcely* and *barely*. See SOONER.

hardy, hearty   *Hardy* means rugged, strong, bold, able to withstand hardship. *Hearty* is cordial, warm, vigorous, robust, abundant, nourishing (*hardy* campers, a *hardy* species, a *hearty* welcome, a *hearty* breakfast, a *hearty* endorsement).

harebrained   giddy, reckless, flighty; not *hairbrained*.

headquarters   can be used with singular or plural verb, although the plural is more common. (Its *headquarters* are in Chicago.) The verb form (They were *headquartered* in Chicago.) is accepted by most current dictionaries but rejected by several usage authorities.

healthful, healthy   *Healthful* is largely restricted to "conducive to good health" (a *healthful* diet). *Healthy's* primary meaning is "possessing good health" (a *healthy* body) but its use as "conducive to good health" (a *healthy* climate) is acceptable. It also may mean considerable, vigorous (a *healthy* yell, a *healthy* portion).

heap, heaps   informal when used to mean a great number or large amount (a *heap* of love, *heaps* of money).

Frederic had inherited heaps of money.

hearty   See HARDY, HEARTY.

heir apparent, heir presumptive   An *heir apparent* is one whose right to property or title cannot be denied on the death of the ancestor. An *heir presumptive* is in line for such an inheritance but could lose it if someone more closely related to the ancestor is born.

hence, whence   *From hence* is considered archaic and *from whence* redundant. *Hence* means from this time, after now, for this reason, therefore (a year *hence*, The car's springs were bad; *hence* the rough ride.). *Whence* means from what origin, source or cause. (I know not *whence* he came.)

hiccup, hiccough   *Hiccup* is the prevailing form, though *hiccough* is not unacceptable.

high, highly   As an adverb, *high* is usually used to indicate distance up, both literally and figuratively. (I jumped *high*. I rose *high* in the agency.) *Highly* is normally used in a figurative sense (*highly* placed officials, *highly* successful) and as an intensive (*highly* amusing).

hinder   Its main preposition is *from*. (The rain *hindered* me *from* completing my project in the yard.) See PREVENT, HINDER.

hint   most often uses the preposition *at*. (He *hinted at* his next move.)

historic, historical   *Historic* refers to something that stands out in history (the *historic* battle at Gettysburg, a *historic* building). *Historical* applies to something concerned with history, whether it stands out or not (a *historical* novel, a *historical* king). The words are preceded by *a* or *an*, whichever you are comfortable with.

hitchhike, hitchhiker   double *h*.

hitherto   until now, up to this time. (The market has reached heights *hitherto* believed impossible.) Do not use this for "until then" or "until that time," as in "In 1985, the market reached heights *hitherto* believed impossible." Use "previously," or even "theretofore."

hoard, horde   A *hoard* is a supply or accumulation stored away (a *hoard* of money, a *hoard* of food). A *horde* is a large group or crowd, a swarm (a *horde* of bargain hunters, a *horde* of locusts).

hog   See PIG, HOG.

hoi polloi   The masses, the common people. "*The hoi polloi*" is frowned on by some usage guides because *hoi* means *the* in Greek, a distinction that is largely ignored, notably by current dictionaries.

holocaust   great or total destruction, especially by fire and usually with extensive loss of life (nuclear *holocaust*). Capitalize *Holocaust*, for Adolf Hitler's slaughter of Jews and others during World War II.

hoofs, hooves   *Hoofs* is a heavy preference over *hooves* for the plural. The participles are *hoofed* and *hoofing*.

hopefully   Usage guides say this means "in a hopeful manner" and should not be used to mean "it is hoped." However, the sense of "it is hoped" is recognized by recent dictionaries, though some caution that you may wish to avoid it.

host   The use of *host* as a verb is condemned by many usage commentators but is accepted by most current dictionaries (*hosted* the meeting).

hurdle, hurtle   To *hurdle* is to leap over a barrier, to overcome, to surmount a difficulty, a problem, etc. (*hurdled* the last obstacle). To *hurtle* is to move violently, with great speed. (The car *hurtled* across the median into three lanes of oncoming traffic.)

hyperbole   an intentional exaggeration that is used for emphasis and is not intended to be taken literally, as "You look like a million dollars" or "My feet weigh a ton" or "I'd sell my soul for that car."

hyper-, hypo-   *Hyper-* is a prefix meaning excessive, over, above, beyond, abnormal (*hypersensitive, hyperactive*). *Hypo-* means below, beneath, under, less than normal, deficient (*hypodermic, hypoglycemia*). The prefixes are sometimes confused, as is often the case with *hyperthermia* (unusually high fever) and *hypothermia* (subnormal body temperature).

I

-ics   When words ending in *-ics* (such as *statistics*, *tactics*, *acoustics*) refer to a science, art, skill, subject, etc., they take a singular verb. (*Politics* is the subject of tonight's lecture.) When they apply to practical activities or qualities, they are plural. (Their *politics* were disturbing to their friends.)

identical   takes preposition *with* or *to*. (Your shirt is *identical to* mine. Your car is *identical with* mine.)

identify   When a preposition is needed, *identify* usually takes *with* (*identified with* a conservative organization). It often takes a reflexive pronoun (*identified themselves* with the movie's hero), but in most cases it can be omitted.

idiosyncrasy   not *idiosyncracy*.

idle   accepted as a transitive verb meaning "to make idle, to cause to be inactive." (The strike *idled* hundreds of workers.)

i.e.   See E.G., I.E.

if, whether   Either may introduce a noun clause, usually following verbs such as see, ask, learn, doubt, know, and wonder: (I doubt *if* [or *whether*] they know the answer.) Avoid ambiguities such as "Let them know *if* they are selected." *Whether* is often required when alternatives are involved. (I don't know *whether* to laugh or cry.)

if and when   Pick the one most appropriate to the context; you don't usually need them both. (We will make our decision *if and when* [when] the report arrives. We will ask about the missing documents *if and when* [if] she takes the stand.)

ignoramus   Its plural is *ignoramuses*, not *ignorami*.

ilk   a Scots term meaning of the same place, estate, or name. "Campbell of that *ilk*" means "Campbell of Campbell." *Ilk* is now legitimately used almost exclusively for *sort* or *kind* (attorney Jones and others of his *ilk*, and other books of that *ilk*).

ill used with the preposition *with* (*ill with* pneumonia). *Ill of* is not incorrect but it is rarely seen.

illicit See ELICIT, ILLICIT.

illusion See DELUSION, ILLUSION.

imaginary, imaginative *Imaginary* is not real, existing only in the imagination (an *imaginary* illness, the child's *imaginary* friend). *Imaginative* is characterized by or showing imagination (*imaginative* plans for the new hall, *imaginative* use of recycled plastics).

Clara waited for her imaginary friend, Lydia, to throw the ball.

immature, premature *Immature* is emotionally undeveloped, unripe, not fully grown (*immature* behavior). *Premature* is mature or ripe before the proper time or coming too soon. (The decision was *premature*. He was *prematurely* gray.)

immigrate See EMIGRATE, IMMIGRATE.

imminent See EMINENT, IMMINENT.

immoral See AMORAL, IMMORAL.

immune Its usual prepositions are *from* and *to* (*immune from* taxation, *immune to* criticism).

immunity, impunity *Immunity* means exempt or protected from a disease, duty, service, obligation, harm, liability, punishment, etc. (*immunity* from taxation, *immunity* to smallpox). *Impunity* also means exempt but applies only to penalty or other undesirable consequences. (You can't run red traffic lights with *impunity*.)

immure, inure *Immure* means to shut up within or as if within walls, to entomb in a wall, imprison, enclose. (She *immured* herself in the tiny room to work on the project.) It is occasionally used erroneously for *inure*, which means to make or become accustomed to something difficult or unpleasant (*inured* to the harsh climate).

impact   Its use as a verb, meaning to have an effect on (They will study how the closing of the plant *impacted* the tiny community.), is criticized by most usage guides, but most of my dictionaries have no problem with it. *Impact* is accepted as a noun meaning effect or influence. (The project had little *impact* on the school.)

impassable, impassible, impassive *Impassable* means something cannot be passed, crossed, traveled, or surmounted. (The road was *impassable*.) *Impassible* means incapable of suffering pain or experiencing emotion (the *impassible* prisoner). *Impassive* means showing no emotion. (I wondered what lay behind that *impassive* face.)

impatiens   This plant's name is easily misspelled, probably because it sounds like *impatience*.

impeach   to bring formal charges against a public official. It is not a conviction or a removal from office. Under the U.S. Constitution, the House of Representatives *impeaches* a president, who is then tried by the Senate, where a two-thirds vote of the senators present is required for a finding of guilty. The senators may then remove the president from office or decide on some other punishment.

impervious   Its preposition is almost always *to*. (My hat was *impervious to* water. She was *impervious to* their threats.)

implicit   most often followed by the preposition *in*. (The gravity of the situation was *implicit in* the statement.)

imply, infer   To *imply* is to suggest, to hint, to state indirectly. (The prosecutor *implied* that the defense attorney was grandstanding.) To *infer* is to conclude, to deduce. (The defense attorney *inferred* from the prosecutor's remarks that he was being accused of grandstanding.) *Infer* is sometimes used erroneously in the sense of *imply*. This meets strong opposition from usage authorities and dictionaries.

important, importantly   Both forms are acceptable as adverbs modifying sentences and are ordinarily used with *more* or *most*. More (most) *important* is preferred. (*Most important*, I lost my keys. *More importantly*, we won the game.)

impose   Its preposition is usually *on*, and far less frequently, *upon*. (I don't want to *impose on* your hospitality. A tax increase was *imposed on* gasoline.)

impostor   *Impostor* is the spelling preferred to *imposter*. The word refers to a person who pretends to be someone or something he is not.

impresario   frequently misspelled *impressario*.

impress   uses a number of prepositions, depending on the context. Among them: *by* (*impressed by* their courage), *with* (*impressed with* the view), *on* or *upon* (*impressed on* them the need for caution), and *in* or *into* (*impressed* the prisoners *into* the navy).

impromptu   See EXTEMPORANEOUS, IMPROMPTU.

improve   followed almost always by *on* or *upon*. (It's hard to *improve on* perfection.)

impunity   See IMMUNITY, IMPUNITY.

inability, disability   *Inability* is the lack of ability, power, or resources to do something (their *inability* to score in clutch situations). *Disability* is a lack of strength or physical or mental ability, a permanent flaw, an incapacity that prevents someone from doing something (received a pension because of a physical *disability*).

in addition to   See TOGETHER WITH.

incentive   most often followed by *to*. (The bonus was offered as an *incentive to* renewed effort. The promise of prize money provided an *incentive to* improve our skills.) It is sometimes followed by *for*. (The prospect of raises was an *incentive for* reducing mistakes.)

incident   a minor occurrence or happening. It should not be used to describe a major event, such as an earthquake or an airliner crash involving great loss of life. It is often applied to an occurrence connected to a more important event (just one *incident* in a long career) or an apparently minor event that could lead to serious consequences (a border *incident*, an international *incident*).

incidental   most often used with the preposition *to* (problems *incidental* to the job).

incidentally   aside from the main subject, by the way, in an incidental manner. (*Incidentally*, I landed the Bloomberg contract today.) *Incidently* is considered an incorrect spelling.

include   applies to part of a larger whole. (The five-member committee *includes* representatives of labor and management.) Do not use *include* when you list all of the components; say, "Members of the group are..." or "The commission comprises...."

incongruous   most commonly followed by *with*. (His actions were *incongruous with* his principles.)

incorporate   usually followed by *in* or *into*. (Your ideas have been *incorporated into* the proposal.) *With* is sometimes used.

incredible, incredulous   unbelievable, hard to believe. (The escape was *incredible*.) *Incredulous* means disbelieving, skeptical. (An *incredulous* jury rejected the defendant's explanation.)

inculcate   Its principal prepositions are *in* or *into*. (They *inculcated* virtue *in* the young students.) *With* is also used. (The students were *inculcated with* the principles of virtue.)

incumbent   Its prepositions are most often *on* or *upon,* usually followed by an infinitive. (It is *incumbent upon* you to speak out.)

independent   Its preposition is *of* (*independent of* the board's advice).

index   plural is *indexes*. *Indices* is acceptable but rarely used.

indict   See CHARGE, INDICT, ARRAIGN.

indifferent   most often followed by the preposition *to*. (He was *indifferent to* the plight of his tenants.)

indispensable   not *indispensible*.

indulge   used as an intransitive verb usually followed by *in* (*indulged in* a day at the track). The transitive form uses *in* and *with* (*indulged* myself *in* an extra hour's sleep, *indulged* my wife *with* a small gift").

inedible, uneatable Both are used for something that is not suitable for eating, though *uneatable* is seldom used.

infectious See CONTAGIOUS, INFECTIOUS.

infer See IMPLY, INFER.

inferior, superior Both take the preposition *to*, not *than*. (Smith is *superior to* Jones.)

infest most often followed by *with* (an *apartment infested* with rats) and less frequently *by*. (The woods were *infested by* snakes.)

infiltrate Its preposition is *into*. (Agents are *infiltrating into* the mob's smuggling operation.)

inflame proper version. It has a variant, *enflame*, that is rarely seen.

inflammable See FLAMMABLE, INFLAMMABLE.

inflict, afflict *Inflict* takes *on* or *upon* and its object is punishment, pain, or whatever else is being inflicted. *Afflict* takes *with* or *by* and its object is the person or persons being afflicted. (The military *inflicts* harsh punishment upon deserters. The community was *afflicted with* an outbreak of typhoid fever.)

infuse usually followed by *with* in the sense of imbue, inspire. (The boss *infused* the staff *with* a sense of purpose.) It is followed by *into* in the sense of instill. (The boss *infused* a sense of purpose *into* the staff.)

ingenious, ingenuous, disingenuous The similarity in spelling appears to confuse some people. *Ingenious* means clever, inventive, imaginative, resourceful (an *ingenious* idea for sorting trash). *Ingenuous* means candid, innocent, open, artless, naive. (The child's testimony was *ingenuous*.) *Disingenuous* means insincere, not frank or candid.

The candidate's explanation was disingenuous.

inhuman, unhuman *Inhuman* means barbarous, cruel, savage, etc. (the *inhuman* treatment of the prisoners). It is also used frequently in the sense of *unhuman*, which means not human, not possessing human characteristics. (The face that appeared in the window was *unhuman*.)

inimical   harmful, hostile, adverse. Its preposition is *to*. (My doctor says smoking is *inimical to* my health.)

in, into   *Into* is the word of preference with verbs of motion or change when the direction is from the outside to a point within, although *in* is often used in this sense. *Into* is the best word in these cases. (He leaped *into* the room. The car roared *into* the parking lot and slammed *into* the wall.) Use *in* to say, "Go jump *in* the lake." "Split *in* two." "Spit *in* the ocean." Beware of constructions like "He turned himself *into* police (*in to*)."

innocent   The plea *not guilty* is preferred to *innocent*, especially in legal circles. *Innocent* is the style at many newspapers because of the ease with which *not* in *not guilty* can be dropped.

innocuous   sometimes misspelled *inocuous*.

innovation   something newly introduced—an idea, device, method of doing things; *new innovation* is redundant—and watch the spelling.

inoculate   often misspelled with two *n*'s.

in order to   usually, *in order* is not necessary. "I circled the block *in order* to avoid a left turn at the busy intersection" can be shortened to "I circled the block *to* avoid …"

inquire, enquire   *Enquire* is seldom used. The two words use the prepositions *about, into, after,* and *for*. (He *inquired about* the car. The board will *inquire into* the incident. I *inquired after* Joe [asked about his well-being]. I stopped by the store and *inquired for* Smith [asked to see him].)

inroad, inroads   The prepositions are chiefly *into* and *on*. The plural is usually used, especially when the meaning is encroachment or an advance at another's expense. (Foreign companies are making *inroads into* the American textile market.)

insensible   usually takes the prepositions *to* and *of* (*insensible to* the cold, *insensible of* our feelings).

inseparable   Its preposition is *from*. (Budget planning is *inseparable from* the strategy for reducing the deficit.)

inside of   well established in American English usage, but in most cases *inside* sounds better. It's more acceptable in reference to time. (I'll be there *inside of* a week.)

insignia, insigne   *Insignia* may be treated as a singular or plural, and the plural *insignias* is also standard. (Their *insignia* was a swastika. The captain's *insignia* were tarnished.) The Latin singular *insigne* is rarely seen.

instill   usually followed by *in* or *into* (*instilling* a sense of duty *into* the troops, *instilling* a love of animals *in* the children). *Instil* is an accepted variant spelling, but it is seldom used in the United States.

instruct   usually followed by *in* when it means teach or educate (*instructed* a class *in* literature) and *to* plus infinitive when it means direct or order (*instructed* them *to* ignore the request).

insure   See ENSURE, INSURE.

intelligent, intellectual   An *intelligent* person has the capacity for learning, reasoning, and understanding. An *intellectual* has all these qualities plus a distinct taste and capacity for higher knowledge.

intense, intensive   *Intense* means to a high degree, strong, acute, severe, great, strenuous, emotional, etc. (*intense* heat, *intense* sunlight, an *intense* person). *Intensive* is sometimes used in some of these senses but additionally it means concentrated on a narrow area (*intensive* care, *intensive* study, *intensive* bombardment).

intent   The adjective *intent's* preposition is *on* (*intent on* their work).

intention   Its most common prepositions are *of*, usually followed by a gerund or a noun (I have no *intention of* leaving. The *intention of* the treaty is to end the war.) and *to* followed by an infinitive. (They announced their *intention to* buy the store.)

intercede   usually followed by *with, for, on,* or *in*. (They *interceded with* the authorities *on* my behalf. They *interceded on* my behalf. The mayor *interceded in* the garbage strike. They *interceded for* the suspect.)

internecine   mutually destructive, involving conflict within a group; characterized by slaughter. (The two political leaders were locked in an *internecine* struggle for control of the party. The *internecine* war was fought between the states.)

interpretative, interpretive   Both adjectives are acceptable.

introduce   takes the prepositions *to* and *into*. (My guide *introduced* me *to* a new restaurant. They *introduced* a serious note *into* the conversation.)

intrude   uses prepositions *on, upon*, and *into* (*intruded on* a private discussion, *intruded upon* a lovers' meeting, the reporter's opinions that *intruded into* the news account of the investigation).

inundate   Its main preposition is *with*. (The television station was *inundated with* telephone calls after the show.) Sometimes it uses *by* (*inundated by* the swollen creek).

inure, enure   *Inure* is preferred over its variant, *enure*. Its preposition is usually *to*. (Growing up in Alaska *inured* him *to* harsh temperatures.) See IMMURE, INURE.

invent   See DISCOVER, DEVELOP, INVENT.

invest   *Invest* is usually followed by *in* or *with*, depending on the context. (They *invested* heavily *in* energy stocks. He was *invested with* the full power of the office.)

invite   use of *invite* as a noun is widely criticized as informal or colloquial.

involve   usually followed by *in* (*involved in* politics) or *with* (romantically *involved with* my boss).

iridescent   sometimes misspelled *irridescent*.

irregardless   double negative. Variously labeled as nonstandard, dialectical, illiterate, and a barbarism. Use *regardless* when you want a synonym for heedless or unmindful.

irrelevant   sometimes misspelled *irrevelant*.

iterate, reiterate   Both mean to say or do something over and over again, but *reiterate* implies an insistent or tiring, boring, tedious effect. (The complaint was *reiterated* so often that the board would no longer listen.)

it's, its   These words are continually confused. *It's* is a contraction meaning *it is* or *it has*. (It's been fun.) *Its* is the possessive of *it*. (The team gave *its* all.)

It's me   *It's me* is generally accepted in informal speech, but for hard-nosed writing and formal speech, the choice is *It is I.*

J

jargon See ARGOT, JARGON.

jealous usually followed by *of*. (I was *jealous of* their success. The colonists were *jealous of* their newly won freedom.)

jeer Its usual preposition is *at*. (The crowed *jeered at* the visiting team.)

jibe See GIBE, JIBE.

join uses prepositions *to*, *with*, and *in*. (My gambling debts, *joined to* an increase in rent, contributed to my insolvency. I *joined with* my brothers to form a corporation. They *joined in* singing the chorus.)

join together An idiom widely used informally as an emphatic phrase; often criticized as redundant.

judge advocate plural is *judge advocates*. Also: *judge advocates general*.

judgment spelled *judgment* in the United States, *judgement* in England. However, it's *judgeship* in both.

judicial, judicious *Judicial* pertains to courts, judges, or their functions (the *judicial* system) and the proper character of a judge, especially involving fairness and impartiality (*judicial* bearing). *Judicious* means wise, prudent, showing sound judgment (a *judicious* choice of wine).

jukebox Its most common construction is one word.

juncture *Juncture* is used chiefly to denote a critical point in time, a turning point, a serious convergence of events. (At this *juncture*, we must decide whether to continue with our original strategy or to try another approach.)

jurist, judge A *jurist* is a person who is versed in the law, such as a judge, lawyer, or legal scholar. *Jurist* is not a precise synonym of *judge*, although a *judge* is usually a *jurist*—or should be.

just   exactly, precisely (*just* right), barely (I *just* made it.), only, merely (It's *just* me.), only a moment ago (They *just* left.), and at a little distance (*just* down the road), among other things.

just deserts   When you receive the reward or punishment that you deserve, you get your *just deserts*. The phrase has nothing to do with food, although the noun is frequently misspelled *desserts*.

K

karat   See CARAT, KARAT, CARET.

ketchup   This spelling is preferred to *catchup* or *catsup*.

kilt, kilts   The Scottish garment for men is a *kilt*, singular, not *kilts*. (The bagpiper wore a kilt.)

kindergarten   *kindergarten* and *kindergartner,* not *kindergarden* or *kindergardner.*

kindly   standard when used to mean please, as a matter of courtesy, as a polite request or demand. (*Kindly* close the door. *Kindly* remit. Would you *kindly* fill out this form and return it to me?)

kitty-cornered   See CATER-CORNERED.

kneeled, knelt   Both words are acceptable as the past tense and participle of *kneel*, but *knelt* is a strong preference. (They *knelt* at the altar.)

knickknack   not *knicknack.*

knit   Its past tense and past participle are either *knit* or *knitted* (*knitted* his brow, loosely/tightly *knit*).

knot   a unit of speed equal to one nautical mile per hour. It's incorrect to say *knots per hour.*

know-how   hyphenated; knowledge to do something well, expertise, technical skill.

kowtow   accepted spelling.

kudos   a Greek word meaning praise or glory; the *s* does not mean it is plural. It is a singular noun that takes a singular verb: *kudos is*, not *kudos are*.

L

lack for   an acceptable phrase; almost always appears with negatives. (We don't *lack for* friends. The lawyers didn't *lack for* ammunition to support their case.)

lacerations   See ABRASIONS, LACERATIONS, CONTUSIONS.

laden   usually takes the preposition *with* (*laden with* cares, a cart *laden with* pots).

lag   usually followed by *behind*. (The company's production *lagged behind* its rival's. The boy *lagged behind* his father.)

lama, llama   A *lama* is a Buddhist monk; a *llama* is a South American beast of burden that is also the source of a soft fleece.

lament   uses the prepositions *about, for*, or *over*. (She *lamented about* her unfair treatment. We *lamented for* our father. They *lamented over* the loss of their meeting room.)

larboard   See PORT, STARBOARD, LARBOARD.

last, latest   use *latest* rather than *last* when *last* may suggest a finality that is not meant, as in "His last offer was for $20,000." But use *last* to denote "next before the present" (*last* week, *last* spring, *last* Christmas).

latter   See FORMER, LATTER.

laudable, laudatory   *Laudable* is deserving praise and *laudatory* is expressing praise (their *laudable* effort, a *laudatory* report).

laugh   usually followed by *at*. (We *laughed at* the clown.) It is sometimes followed by *over*. (We still *laugh over* the problem the kids had during last year's trip.)

lawman   a standard term for a law-enforcement officer, especially a sheriff, marshal, or police officer.

lawyer See ATTORNEY, LAWYER.

lay, lie The two verbs are often misused. *Lay* is a transitive verb that means "to put or place." Its past participle is *laid*, and its present participle is *laying*. (I am *laying* the book on the table. I *laid* the book on the table. I have *laid* the book on the table.) *Lie*, an intransitive verb, means to assume a reclining position. Its past tense is *lay*. Its present participle is *lying* and past participle *lain*. (I am *lying* on the sofa. I *lay* on the sofa for a few minutes. I have *lain* on the sofa.)

lead, led The past tense and past participle of the verb *lead* is *led*, which frequently is incorrectly written *lead*—probably because of confusion with the metal *lead*, which is pronounced *led*. (*Lead* the way. We *led* the way. My feet felt like *lead*.)

leaped, leapt Both forms are acceptable for the past tense and past participle of *leap*. (I *leaped* to my feet. I *leapt to* my feet.)

learn, teach The use of *learn* for *teach* is nonstandard. Instead of "That'll *learn* you to mess with my stuff," say, "That'll *teach* you to mess with my stuff."

leastways, leastwise These two words mean at least or at any rate. *Leastways* is considered dialectal and *leastwise* informal or colloquial. (*Leastwise* [or *leastways*], that's what he told me.)

leave, let alone Interchangeable when the sense is "don't disturb." (*Leave* [or *let*] them alone.) The use of *leave* for *let* in all other senses is not acceptable. (*Let* us pray. *Let* it go.)

lectern, podium, dais A *lectern* is a stand with a slanted top on which speakers place their books and notes, a *podium* is a raised platform for a lecturer or orchestra conductor, and a *dais* is a raised platform for a lectern, table, honored guests, or speakers.

led See LEAD, LED.

leery, leary *Leery* is treated as standard by most recent desk dictionaries. It is usually followed by *of*. (I'm *leery of* people who offer unsolicited advice.) *Leary* is a variant that is rarely used.

lend, loan   *Loan* is acceptable as a verb, particularly in business usage. *Lend* is preferred in most figurative phrases. (*Lend* me a hand. *Lend* an ear.)

lengthy   conveys the idea of something excessively long and drawn out that *long* does not. It is often used to describe a speech, writing, or a program or other event (a *lengthy* journey, a *lengthy* sermon, a *lengthy* trial).

less   See FEWER, LESS.

lesser   a comparative of *little* that means smaller in size, value, or importance (the *lesser* of two evils, a *lesser* person, the *lesser* of the two, the *lesser* distance).

let   See LEAVE, LET.

level   followed by prepositions *at* when it means *aim* (*leveled* criticism *at* the plan) and *with* when it means be open or frank. (They *leveled with* us.) Some dictionaries label the open or frank sense as informal or slang.

liable   uses the preposition *for* when it means responsible or obligated (*liable for* your partner's debts), *to* when it means susceptible or subject (*liable to* felony charges), and *to* with infinitive when it means apt or likely. (You're *liable to* fall.)

liaison   often misspelled.

libel, slander   *Libel* is a written, printed, or pictorial statement, rather than oral, that damages a person's reputation or character. *Slander* is false oral defamation.

lie   See LAY, LIE.

lief   an oldie that means gladly or willingly and is used with *would as* or *had as*. (I would as *lief* eat out tonight.)

life-size   *Life-size* is the predominant construction, though *life-sized* is not wrong.

lighted, lit   These forms are equally acceptable as past tense and past participle of *light*. *Lighted* may be more common for the participle, especially as an attributive, and *lit* more common for the past tense. (I *lit* the cigarette. I held a *lighted* cigarette.) But the following is correct: a *moonlit* night, a *starlit* sky.

It hit him like a
bolt of lightning.

lightening, lightning   *Lightening* is lessening the load or making or becoming not so dark, and *lightning* is a bolt from the blue. (*Lightening* the load made it possible to drive the truck up the hill. *Lightning* struck a block away.)

likable   *Likeable* is a variant that is not commonly used.

like See TOGETHER WITH.

likely   As an adverb meaning probably, *likely* is often preceded by a qualifying word such as *quite, more, most,* or *rather*. (She *most likely* will accept the position. They *quite likely* will approve the changes.)

liken   followed by the preposition *to*. (People *liken* my car to a tank.)

linage, lineage   *Linage* applies to printed lines and *lineage* to ancestry (the newspaper's declining *linage*, a dog of uncertain *lineage*). Most dictionaries also give *lineage* as a variant of *linage*.

liquefy   not *liquify*; means to become liquid or to cause to become liquid (*liquefied* petroleum gas).

litany   a prayer that involves a series of invocations followed by responses. Figuratively, it is a prolonged, repetitive, monotonous recitation. (She had a *litany* of complaints. The serial killer's criminal history was a *litany* of horror.) It is sometimes confused with *liturgy*, a prescribed form of public worship.

literally, figuratively   *Literally* means to the letter; exactly as stated. Often misused as an intensifier meaning *in effect*. "He *literally* took food out of the children's mouths" would suggest hands in small throats. The sense intended belongs to *figuratively*, a metaphorical device that means "in a manner of speaking." (The storm *literally* blew the house off its foundation.) *Literally* is not necessary here.

lit   See LIGHTED, LIT.

livable   preferred to *liveable*.

livid   from a Latin word meaning black and blue, as a bruise, then developed the meaning of ashen, pallid. From there, it picked up the meaning of furiously angry, as in "*livid* [pale] with rage," and then gained the sense of reddish or flushed, which is the way some angry people look. Now *livid* is used primarily in reference to anger and less commonly to describe color.

llama   See LAMA, LLAMA.

loan   See LEND, LOAN.

loath, loathe, loathsome   *Loath* means unwilling, reluctant, disinclined, usually followed by an infinitive (*loath* to accept blame, *loath* to offer an endorsement). To l*oathe* is to detest, hate, abhor. (They *loathe* their boss.) *Loathsome* is disgusting, revolting, repulsive, detestable (a *loathsome* disease).

locate   accepted for discover (We *located* the missing vehicle.), set up in a place (They *located* the business downtown.), settle (The family *located* in Chicago.), and situated. (The house was *located* at Third and Jefferson.) *Locate* is often unnecessary when used for *situated* (was at Third and Jefferson).

loud, loudly   *Loud* sees limited use as an adverb (Don't talk so loud.) but in most constructions *loudly* is preferred. (The crowd cheered *loudly*; The choir sang *loudly*.)

luxuriant, luxurious   *Luxuriant* means growing abundantly, vigorously, such as foliage, hair, beard, crops, etc. *Luxurious* means characteristic of luxury (a *luxurious* home, dinner, lifestyle, etc.). Some dictionaries allow *luxuriant* as a synonym for *luxurious*, but this use is not common.

M

mad, angry *Mad* as a synonym of *angry* has usage commentators and dictionaries almost evenly divided. Perhaps it is best to avoid it in serious speech and writing.

madding, maddening It's *madding* in the quote from Thomas Gray's "Elegy Written in a Country Churchyard"—"Far from the madding crowd's ignoble strife…," and in the title of the work more than a century later by Thomas Hardy, *Far from the Madding Crowd*. It means frenzied, raving, acting as if mad. It is often misused as *maddening*, which means driving mad, making insane, irritating.

magic, magical As an adjective, *magic* is used mostly attributively (the *magic* touch, a *magic* solution); *magical* is used both attributively (a *magical* moment, a *magical* night), and predicatively. (The transformation was *magical*.)

Magna Carta, Magna Charta Both *Carta* and *Charta* are correct, but *Magna Carta* is the more common choice.

majority, plurality *Majority* applies to more than half of a total. A candidate who receives more than half of the votes cast has received a *majority*. If candidate Jones receives 50 votes and candidate Smith receives 30, Jones has a *majority*. In a contest involving three candidates or more, *plurality* applies to the number of votes received by one candidate over the next highest candidate's total. If the contest cited above had a third candidate who received 25 votes, Jones would have received a *plurality* of 20.

manageable not *managable*.

mania, phobia A *mania* is an intense desire or enthusiasm for something, a craze (a *mania* for bridge). A *phobia* is a persistent, illogical fear of something (*claustrophobia, agoraphobia*). Sometimes *phobia* is used where *mania* is intended.

mantel, mantle A *mantel* is a structure around a fireplace, usually having a ledge. A *mantle* is a cloak. Dictionaries allow *mantle* as a variant of *mantel*.

marionette See PUPPET, MARIONETTE.

marital, martial The chances are great for a typographical error that could change either of these words to the other. *Marital* applies to marriage, *martial* to warfare.

marshal not *marshall*. Noun and verb forms: *marshal, marshals, marshaled, marshaling*. However, the proper noun is usually *Marshall*.

martyr The noun is usually followed by *to* (a *martyr* to the cause, a *martyr* to arthritis), and the verb usually takes *for* (*martyred* for his beliefs).

masterful, masterly *Masterful*—imperious, domineering, strong-willed, overpowering (a *masterful* boss)—is sometimes used when the phrase calls for *masterly*, meaning expert, having the skill of a master (a *masterly* performance on the piano). Usage guides and dictionaries are mixed on this practice.

matériel equipment and supplies used by an organization, usually a military force. When used in the military sense, *matériel* applies to a unit's weapons and ammunition, etc. It is distinguished from *personnel*. It should not be confused with *material*. Sometimes spelled without the accent mark: *materiel*. See PERSONNEL.

matinee a dramatic or musical performance presented in the daytime, especially in the afternoon. "Matinee performance" is considered redundant. It is sometimes used with an accent mark: *matinée*.

may See CAN, MAY.

mayoral, mayoralty *Mayoral* is the adjective of *mayor* and *mayoralty* is a noun meaning "the office or term of mayor."

mean See AVERAGE, MEAN, MEDIAN.

means always plural when it refers to resources, available wealth. (We were living beyond our *means*. Their *means* were sufficient.) Plural or singular, depending on the modifier, when it means a method or agency used to obtain an end. (All *means* were used. Every *means* was used.) Most often used with the preposition *of* (finding a *means* of reaching their objective).

meantime, meanwhile   *Meanwhile* and *meantime* are synonyms as both noun (the intervening time) and adverb (in or during the intervening time, at the same time) although *meanwhile* is used more frequently as an adverb and *meantime* sees more use as a noun. (In the *meantime*, we had a couple of drinks. *Meanwhile*, they were posting bail.)

Medal of Honor   The United States' highest military honor. Even though the medal is awarded by Congress, the title does not include "Congressional." It's simply *Medal of Honor.*

media   *Media* is the plural of *medium* when it applies to communications agencies. It does not take a singular verb. (The news *media* were all over that one.) *Mediums* is the plural of *medium* when it refers to those who communicate with the spirits of the dead. *Medias* is incorrect.

median   See AVERAGE, MEAN, MEDIAN.

mediate   Its main preposition is *between*. (We were asked to *mediate between* the union and the company.)

mediator   See ARBITRATOR, MEDIATOR.

meditate   usually followed by *on*. (Let me *meditate on* that idea.) and sometimes *upon*.

melee   sometimes misspelled.

memento   not *momento*. Plural is *mementos* or, infrequently, *mementoes*.

memorandum   Both *memorandums* and *memoranda* are accepted as plurals. *Memorandas* is not. *Memo* is standard.

midnight   refers to an ending day, not one that is beginning. If you participated in a party that began at 8:00 P.M. Friday and lasted four hours, you would have reveled until midnight Friday, not Saturday.

They were mighty happy to see each other again.

mighty   considered informal or colloquial when used as an adverb meaning *very* (a *mighty* fine movie, a *mighty* pleasant person).

migrate   See EMIGRATE, IMMIGRATE, MIGRATE.

militate   most often followed by *against,* on rare occasions *for* or *in favor of.* (Your record *militates against* your credibility.) See MITIGATE, MILITATE.

millennium   *Millenniums* is preferred over *millennia* as the plural. Frequently misspelled. It starts on a one rather than a zero—1001 instead of 1000, 2001 instead of 2000, 3001 instead of 3000—as does a century.

milquetoast   Not *milk toast* for a meek, timid, unassertive person. Derived from a comic strip character. Uppercase or lowercase—*Milquetoast* or *milquetoast.*

mineralogy   Don't spell it *minerology.*

minimal   Do not use *minimal* when you mean just a little or a small amount. It means the minimum, the smallest possible amount or degree. (My interest in international finance is *minimal.*)

minimize   *Minimize* means to reduce to the smallest possible amount or degree, to represent as having the least possible amount, value or importance. (The company *minimized* its losses.) It should not be used for diminish, brush off, underrate or belittle, and it shouldn't be modified with such adverbs as greatly, somewhat, or considerably.

minister   usually followed by *to.* (They *ministered to* the wounded.)

minuscule   very small. Originally referred to a tiny script used in medieval manuscripts. The prefix is *minus-*, not *minis-*. I've seen it misspelled *miniscule* more often than not.

minutia   most often used in the plural, which is *minutiae.* (The talks bogged down in *minutiae.* The *minutiae* have been dealt with.)

mischievous   often misspelled *mischievious* and mispronounced the same way. Pronounced with the accent on the first syllable: MISS-chuv-us.

mishap   See ACCIDENT, MISHAP.

misplace   See DISPLACE, MISPLACE.

misspell   frequently misspelled.

mitigate, militate   *Mitigate*, which means to make or become milder or less severe (Her remorse helped *mitigate* her punishment.) "*Mitigating* circumstances" is sometimes used when the word wanted is *militate*, to have a force or influence or effect *against*. (His strong opinions *militated against* any compromise.) See MILITATE.

mix   mostly followed by *with* (paint *mixed* with water) and sometimes *into*. (Politics got *mixed into* her job with the school system.)

mock   When it needs a preposition, it takes *at*. (They cursed and *mocked at* me.)

moot   In general usage, *moot* means something is arguable, open for discussion or debate. In legal contexts, it applies to something that has become hypothetical or academic. In the first case, a *moot* question is one that is debatable; in legal circles, it is a question that has become insignificant, perhaps because it has already been resolved. When you use this word, make clear which sense you mean. A *moot* court is a mock court where hypothetical cases are tried for the training of students.

moral, morale   *Moral* involves distinction between right and wrong (*moral* code, a question of *morals*), and *morale* applies to the state of a person or group's spirits. (The department's *morale* was high.)

more than one   This phrase takes a singular verb. (Fifteen students took the test, and *more than one* was caught cheating.)

Mormon   a member of the *Church of Jesus Christ of Latter-day Saints*. Note the construction *Latter-day*.

mortician   Like funeral director, *mortician* was born as a euphemism for undertaker. All three are recognized as standard.

Moslem, Muslim   *Muslim* is preferred to *Moslem*, until recently the predominant spelling and still acceptable.

mosquito   preferred plural is *mosquitoes*.

most   See ALMOST, MOST.

mucus, mucous   The noun is *mucus,* the adjective *mucous.*

mull   to consider, ruminate, deliberate; used with *over.* (City officials *mulled over* the proposal for a new office center.)

muse   usually followed by prepositions *on* and *upon.* (We *mused on* our friend's plight.) It less frequently uses *about* or *over.*

Muslim   See MOSLEM, MUSLIM.

mutual, common   *Mutual* applies to a feeling or emotion between two or more persons toward each other (*mutual* respect, *mutual* enemies). The word for something shared by two or more persons is *common*, not *mutual* (*common* interest, *common* knowledge).

myriad   The adjective *myriad* is not followed by *of* (beset by *myriad* problems).

N

naiveté, naïveté, naivete, naivety   Recent American desk dictionaries list *naiveté* first, followed by *naïveté*. Some also allow *naivete*. The British prefer *naivety* but also use *naïveté*.

nary   not any, not one. It is considered regional, dialectical (*nary* a care in the world, *nary* a word did I hear).

nation   See COUNTRY, NATION.

national anthem   Lowercase *the national anthem* but capitalize its title: "The Star-Spangled Banner." Note the hyphen.

nauseated, nauseous   People don't become *nauseous*; they become *nauseated*. Something that is *nauseous* causes people to become *nauseated*. (*Nauseous* fumes made several people ill. Several people were *nauseated* by the foul-smelling gas. The critic said the play was *nauseous*. The critic was *nauseated* by the performance.) There appears to be a growing preference for *nauseating* in the *causing* sense of *nauseous*. (I find the taste of asparagus *nauseating*.)

The admiral contemplated his navel.

navel, naval   *Naval* refers to ships and navies (*naval* strength, *naval* affairs commission). A *navel* is the mark on the abdomen where the umbilical cord was attached. It's the *navel* orange, not *naval*.

necessary   usually followed by *to* (The contribution was *necessary to* the survival of the corporation.) It is sometimes followed by *for*. (Water was *necessary for* their survival.)

necessity   Uses the preposition *of* (the *necessity of* food and clothing), *for* (the *necessity for* clear thinking), and sometimes *to* and infinitive (the *necessity to* finish the job before sundown).

need   Its prepositions are *for* (There is a *need for* our assistance.), *of* (We were in *need of* water.), and *to*. (We have no *need to* wait.)

neglectful   Its preposition is *of* (*neglectful* of their employees).

negligent, negligible   *Negligent* is neglectful, indifferent, inattentive, careless (*negligent* in his official duties). *Negligible* is too unimportant or insignificant to be worth considering. (The saving was *negligible*.)

negotiate   acceptable in the sense of successfully going over or through, surmounting, accomplishing (*negotiated* a sharp curve, *negotiated* the rapids).

neither/nor   See EITHER/OR, NEITHER/NOR.

nerve-racking   producing anxiety, tension, irritation, exasperation. This form is preferred to *nerve-wracking*. The *rack* is from an instrument of torture that stretches; *wrack* means wreck or destroy. The nerves are stretched, not wrecked. See RACK, WRACK

never   See ALMOST NEVER.

New Year's   The most common constructions are *New Year's Eve* and *New Year's Day*. *New Year's* alone is acceptable for *New Year's Day*.

nickel   not *nickle*.

nohow   not acceptable in serious speech or writing for "in no way, not at all, anyway." (It wasn't a good car *nohow*.)

noisome   noxious, disgusting, foul-smelling. (The landfill was the source of a *noisome* odor.) It is related to *annoy* but not *noisy*, for which it is often misused, as in "The *noisome* crowd protested the foul called by the referee."

nolo contendere   a Latin term meaning "I do not wish to contend." It is a plea in which a defendant chooses not to present a defense but does not admit guilt. The defendant may be found guilty and punished by a judge. Such a plea does not forbid a person from denying the charges in collateral proceedings.

none   Generally, *none* takes a singular verb when the meaning is *not one* or *no one*, and plural in most other constructions. (*None* of the boxes was empty. *None* of the people were ready to go home.)

noplace   considered an informal term for *nowhere*.

normalcy, normality   Both terms mean the state or character of being normal, although *normality* is more widely used. Warren G. Harding stirred up the intellectual community when he used *normalcy* during his campaign for president in 1920. However, the word had been around long before Harding used it.

no sooner   It's *no sooner than* rather than *no sooner when*. (I'd *no sooner* arrived home *than* the phone rang.)

notorious   *Notorious,* like famous, noted, notable, etc., means widely known, but for unfavorable reasons (a *notorious thief,* a *notorious* gambler).

not too   Although this phrase used in the sense of *not very* has detractors, it is not incorrect. (I'm *not too* sure I like that idea. Our chances of winning are *not too* good.)

novice   See AMATEUR, NOVICE.

number   See AMOUNT, NUMBER.

number of   When *number* is preceded by *a* it takes a plural verb. (A *number of* people are watching the movies.) When it is preceded by *the*, the verb is singular. (The *number of* people watching the movies is declining.)

O

obedient uses the preposition *to* (*obedient to* my boss).

object usually followed by the preposition *to*. (I *object to* your methods. We *objected to* being second-guessed.)

objet d'art sometimes incorrectly used as *object d'art*.

oblige, obligate Both mean to bind legally or morally (*obligated* [or *obliged*] to pay $50 a month). When the obligation is mainly in the mind of the person involved, the choice is *oblige*. (I felt *obliged* to buy them a Christmas gift.) *Oblige* has other meanings that *obligate* cannot share, among them to place under debt for a favor or service done. (We're *obliged* for the ride.), to do a favor for. (They *obliged* us with a song.)

oblivious forgetful, without remembrance, unaware, heedless, unmindful, unconscious. It takes the prepositions *of* or *to* (*oblivious of* what was happening, *oblivious to* his surroundings).

observance, observation *Observance* is the act of following, conforming to, or making a law or custom (a parade in *observance* of the Fourth of July). *Observation* is noticing, watching, perceiving. (The patient was under *observation*.)

observant followed by *of* (*observant* of the Sabbath).

obsolete, obsolescent *Obsolete* means no longer in use, outmoded, out of date (an *obsolete* word, an *obsolete* warship). Something that is *obsolescent* is in the process of passing out of use, becoming *obsolete* (an *obsolescent* computer program).

obviate to prevent or to make unnecessary. (The dog that bit the child was found, *obviating* a series of painful rabies shots.) It should not be used to mean *remove*, as in "The city *obviated* the roadblocks after a number of complaints were received."

occasion   usually followed by *of* (on the *occasion of* their marriage), *for* (an *occasion* for celebration), or *to* plus the infinitive. (I had *occasion to speak* with them.) It is sometimes misspelled *occassion*.

occupy   most often uses the prepositions *with* (They *occupied* themselves *with* a card game.) and *by*. (I *occupied* myself *by* throwing darts.)

occur   *Occurred* and *occurring* take double *r*, as does *occurrence*, which is sometimes misspelled *occurrance*.

The two octopuses enjoyed their reunion.

octopus   Its main plurals are *octopuses* and *octopi*, with *octopuses* preferred. *Octopodes* is also acceptable but is rarely seen.

odd   should be hyphenated when used to indicate a few more than a given number. (Thirty-*odd* musicians participated.) Without the hyphen, the phrase (30 *odd* musicians) could be taken as a reference to a group of eccentrics. Do not use with a specific number (38-*odd* police officers).

offensive   Its preposition is *to* (mannerisms that were *offensive* to me).

officeholder   one word.

official, officious   The adjective *official* pertains to an office or position of authority, characteristic of officials and bureaucracy (the *official* position, *official* red tape). *Officious* applies to someone who is objectionably aggressive in offering unwanted or unrequested help or advice. (We firmly told the *officious* clerk that we were only browsing.)

off of   frequently used in speech and informal writing, as in "Take your feet off of the coffee table." Usually the *of* can be eliminated.

offspring   used as both a singular and a plural. (Your *offspring* are in the barn. Where's our *offspring*? She'll be here later.) *Offsprings* is hardly ever used.

older   See ELDER, OLDER.

old-time, old-timer   Hyphenate both. But "the good *old times*" is proper."

omission   See OVERSIGHT, OMISSION

one of the . . . if not the   This construction presents a pitfall. (The office center is *one of the* tallest, *if not the* tallest, buildings in the state.) The phrase enclosed in commas requires *building*, singular. Put the noun after the first *tallest*. (The office center is *one of the* tallest buildings in the state, if not the tallest.)

only   *Only* should be placed immediately in front of the word or words it modifies. (We drink *only* coffee, not We *only* drink coffee.) However, if precise placement of the modifier gives you a strained, awkward sentence, put it before the verb. (Their behavior could *only* be described as silly.)

onto, on to   Use as one word when you mean "to a place or position on. (He climbed *onto* the hood of the car.) Use as two words when *on* modifies a verb and *to* is a preposition. (She drove *on to* the next town.)

onward, onwards   Either may be used as an adverb. (They pressed *onward* [or *onwards*].) However, *onward* is preferred. Only *onward* may be used as an attributive adjective (*onward* course).

ophthalmologist, optometrist, optician, oculist   *Ophthalmologists* and *oculists* are medical doctors who deal with the anatomy, functions, and diseases of the eye. Most such practitioners call themselves *ophthalmologists*, a word often misspelled. An *optometrist* examines eyes and prescribes eyeglasses. An *optician* makes glasses as prescribed by an *optometrist* or an *ophthalmologist* and makes and sells optical glass and instruments.

opossum   See POSSUM, OPOSSUM.

opportunity   most often followed by *to* and infinitive (gave me the *opportunity to* know them better) and *for* (provided the *opportunity for* a vacation, presented the *opportunity for* cleaning up some loose ends).

opposition   Its main preposition is *to* (in *opposition to* the Democratic bill).

optimistic   *Optimistic* describes a tendency to look on the more favorable side or to expect the best. (We remained *optimistic* throughout those dark times. We were *optimistic* that we would win the war.) It should not be used as a synonym for *hopeful* or *encouraging*. (The fans were *optimistic* that their team could regain the lead. There were *optimistic* signs that things would improve.)

oral, written, verbal   *Verbal* can apply to something *oral* or *written*. When you are required to be precise, use *oral* for something spoken, and *written* for something on paper. *Verbal* has long been used in the *oral* sense and this presents no problem as long as the context is clear. (Half of the examination was *oral*. We presented a *written* response. Their *verbal* skills were below average. We had no time to prepare documents, so we made a *verbal* request.)

ordinance, ordnance   An *ordinance* is a law, usually municipal, sometimes county. (The aldermen amended the garbage *ordinance*.) *Ordnance* is military weapons, usually cannon and other artillery along with ammunition and equipment. (The sergeant was assigned to an *ordnance* unit.)

Oriental   See ASIAN, ASIATIC, ORIENTAL.

orient, orientate   both are acceptable terms when the meaning is "to familiarize with new surroundings or circumstances," but *orient* is preferred. (The school will *orient* new students on Thursday.)

out loud   interchangeable with *aloud* in general use, though *aloud* is the better choice in more formal situations. (They took turns reading the book *aloud*. We were not permitted to think *out loud*.) But only *out loud* works in these phrases. (For crying *out loud*, I laughed *out loud*.)

outside of   *Outside of* is frequently used for *outside,* even though it is redundant and usually sounds better without the *of*, and to mean except for, aside from. Both senses are disparaged by a number of critics, but American dictionaries accept one sense or the other or both. (They aren't found *outside of* the tropics. *Outside of* John's remarks to Charlene, it was a pleasant meeting.)

overlook   Although a sense of *supervise* is among the definitions of *overlook*, this sense is rarely used lest it be confused with a widely used meaning of *overlook*—to ignore, fail to notice. *Oversight* presents a similar problem when it is used to mean overseer. (The question was brought before the project's *oversight* committee.) See OVERSIGHT, OMISSION.

oversight, omission   An *oversight* is an inadvertent omission, an unintentional failure to notice or consider. (Through an *oversight*, Charlie was not invited to the party.) An *omission* is something left out or neglected, either intentionally or unintentionally. (The lack of a signature on the document was a malicious *omission*.) See OVERLOOK.

overwhelm   used most often with *by* (*overwhelmed by* sorrow) and sometimes *with* (*overwhelmed with* criticism).

P

pair   *Pair* uses a singular verb when the reference is to a single entity. (This *pair* of gloves is too small.) The verb is plural when members of the pair are treated as individuals. (A *pair* of robbers were hunted by the police.) *Pairs* is preferred to *pair* when more than one pair is involved (three *pairs* of scissors).

pajamas, pyjamas   The spelling is *pajamas* in the United States and *pyjamas* in Great Britain.

An artist's palate.

palate, palette, pallet   *Palate* is the roof of the mouth and sense of taste (a cuisine guaranteed to tickle your *palate*). *Palette* is a board with a thumb hole used by an artist to mix colors. *Pallet* is, among other things, a bed or mattress of straw or a portable platform for storing or moving goods. (I slept on a *pallet*. The appliance factory was running out of *pallets*.)

panacea   A remedy for all diseases, ills, or difficulties. Since it is a cure-all for all troubles, it cannot be used for a single disease or problem. You can refer to "a *panacea* for the world's social problems" but not "a *panacea* for child abuse."

pandemic   See ENDEMIC, EPIDEMIC, PANDEMIC.

pander, panderer   As a noun, *panderer* is correct, but *pander* is used more often (a *pander* for the prostitutes on the east side). The intransitive verb *pander* is usually followed by *to* (*pandering to* vulgar tastes).

paparazzo   A photographer, usually freelance, who hounds celebrities in search of candid pictures of them. It is often misspelled. Its plural is *paparazzi*, which appears more often than the singular. The term *paparazzo* sprang from the name of a photographer in the 1960 movie *La Dolce Vita*.

parallel   easily misspelled. Prepositions that follow the adjective are *to* and *with*. (The boat sailed *parallel to* the shoreline. The street runs *parallel with* the interstate.) The noun most often takes *between*. (We noticed *parallels between* the two debaters.) Sometimes it takes *to* (The speaker mentioned a *parallel to* other wars.) and *with*. (They saw a *parallel with* an earlier incident.)

paramount   chief in importance, supreme, preeminent (the *paramount* issue on the agenda) and should not be used as a mere synonym of *first* or *important*.

parasol, umbrella   A *parasol* is a light umbrella carried as a protection against the sun. An *umbrella* protects against both sun and rain, but mostly rain.

pardon, parole, probation   A *pardon* is the release from a penalty granted by a governor or other high official. *Parole* is release, on the condition of good behavior, from a sentence that has not expired. *Probation* is the suspension of a sentence of a person not yet imprisoned; a judge grants probation and can revoke it if its terms are violated and order the defendant to serve the sentence.

parenting   This word is criticized by a number of usage authorities but is given as standard by current dictionaries. It means the rearing of children by parents.

pari-mutuel   The hyphenated version is preferred. It's a form of betting on horse races in which winners divide the total amount wagered in proportion to the sum they bet—minus management's cut.

parliamentarian   *Parliamentarian* is not used to designate a member of a parliament. A *parliamentarian* is a person who is an expert in parliamentary rules and procedures and who may or may not be a member of a parliament. The term applies to the skills, not the membership.

parole   See PARDON, PAROLE, PROBATION.

parricide, patricide   *Parricide* is the act of murdering one's father or mother or any other near relative. *Patricide* is the murder of one's father.

part   The intransitive verb ordinarily uses *from* when the sense is to go away, leave, keep separate (We *parted from* the Smiths in Chicago.) and *with* when the sense is to give up, to relinquish. (I hated to *part with* my money.)

partake   to participate or take a share. When it means participate it takes the preposition *in* (*partake in* a game of pinochle), and when it means take a share it is followed by *of* (to *partake of* a meal). One does not partake alone. The past tense is *partook* and participles are *partaken* and *partaking*.

part and parcel   This phrase denotes an essential part. (The ten-point program was *part and parcel* of Smith's campaign.) It is criticized as verbose by some commentators, who say that "and parcel" should be eliminated, and as a cliche by others, but it is treated as standard in recent desk dictionaries.

partial   followed by *to* when it means to have a liking for, favoring (*partial to* chocolate bars, a ruling *partial to* the defendant).

partiality   usually followed by the preposition *for*. (We have a *partiality for* cherry pie.) Sometimes uses *to* or *toward*.

participate   most often followed by the preposition *in*. (They *participated in* extracurricular activities together.)

partisan   See BIPARTISAN, PARTISAN.

passer-by   The hyphenated version is preferred over *passerby* by most dictionaries. The plural is *passers-by* or *passersby*.

past history   In most cases, the *past* in *past history* is redundant and can be omitted.

pastime   something that helps make spare time pass enjoyably, such as a hobby. It is frequently misspelled.

patient   See PATRON, CUSTOMER, CLIENT.

patricide   See PARRICIDE, PATRICIDE.

patron, customer, client, guest, patient   *Patron* is acceptable for *customer*, although it is more likely to be used in a bar, restaurant, or theater. A *customer* is one who buys goods or services, often on a regular basis, at a drugstore, grocery store, service station, etc., as well as a bar or restaurant. *Client* is reserved for a person who uses a professional service, especially from a person such as a lawyer, an architect, or an accountant, or from a government bureau such as a welfare agency. The usual term for people who stay in a hotel is *guest*. A *patient* is one who is under the care of a doctor.

pavilion   not *pavillion*.

peculiar   usually followed by the preposition *to* when it means characteristic of or belonging exclusively to (a saying *peculiar to* the southern United States).

pedal, peddle   To *pedal* is to operate a bicycle, sewing machine, etc. To *peddle* is to sell something.

pejorative   disparaging, derogatory, making or becoming worse. In grammar, *pejorative* refers to a word whose meaning over the course of time has become less favorable or less respectable.

people, persons   Some usage authorities would have you use *persons* for a small or exact number of individuals and *people* for a large, uncounted number. (Thirteen *persons* attended the meeting. Thousands of *people* signed the petitions.) However, you may safely use *people* in place of *persons* in many instances, though there are times when *persons* cannot substitute for *people*. (Five *people* [or *persons*] gathered.) But: (The *people* [not *persons*] won't comply with the new regulations.) Nor would you refer to "one *people*."

perfectly   Acceptable as an intensifier meaning completely, fully. (Let me make this *perfectly* clear.)

periodic, periodical   These are interchangeable in the sense of "occurring at regular intervals." *Periodical* alone pertains to publications that appear at regular intervals—weekly, monthly, etc.

permeate   usually followed by the prepositions *with* and *by*. (The hall was *permeated with* a sense of hopelessness. The locker-room was *permeated by* gloom.)

pernickety   See PERSNICKETY, PERNICKETY.

perquisite, prerequisite   A *perquisite* (*perk* for short) is a payment or privilege in addition to regular pay that is customary or expected, and its preposition is *of*. (The car is a *perquisite of* the position.) A *prerequisite* is a condition required beforehand. Followed usually by *for* or *to* and occasionally by *of*. (A degree is a *prerequisite for* a job with General Widgets Corp. Certain skills are *prerequisite to* promotion.)

persecute, prosecute   To *persecute* is to persistently harass, torment, annoy, often because of religion, race, or beliefs. (Nero *persecuted* the early Christians.) To *prosecute* is to pursue charges in a court of law. (Violators will be *prosecuted*.)

perseverance   Notice the spelling; not *perserverance*.

persnickety, pernickety   *Persnickety* is the preferred American spelling, *pernickety* the British spelling. It's labeled informal or colloquial in dictionaries and means fastidious, fussy, precise, too particular (the *persnickety* customer).

persona   refers to an individual's public image or mask presented to or perceived by the public. (Close aides said the senator's *persona* was misleading.) Also used for a character in a novel or play, sometimes one assumed by the author.

personnel   refers to a group of employees or soldiers. It takes a singular or plural verb. (Our *personnel* are treated well. *Personnel* is no problem here.) Do not use it with a number, as in "Six *personnel* were fired." See MATERIEL.

persons   See PEOPLE, PERSONS.

persuade   See CONVINCE, PERSUADE.

pertinent   Its preposition is *to*. (You must keep your remarks *pertinent to* the matter under discussion.)

peruse   Its meanings range from "read thoroughly, with great care" to "read in a casual or leisurely manner," so make sure your intention is clear. (Charlie quickly *perused* the sports section. It took more than two days to *peruse* the voluminous report.)

pervert   usually followed by *into, to*, and *by*. (The bowling league was *perverted by* its officers *into* a social club. The board *perverted* the program *by* revising its mission. The boss *perverted* my idea *to* a shell of what I intended.)

phenomenon, phenomena   *Phenomenon* is the singular and *phenomena* is its preferred plural. *Phenomenons* is acceptable as a plural. Do not use *phenomena* as a singular or *phenomenas* as a plural.

Philippines   The Republic of the Philippines may be referred to as *the Philippines* or the *Philippine Islands*. The people are *Filipinos*. The adjectives are *Philippine* for the nation (the *Philippine* economy) and *Filipino* for the people (a *Filipino* gathering place). The official language is *Pilipino* (based on Tagalog), along with English.

phony, phoney   *Phony* is the form used most often in American English. The term is considered informal or colloquial by most dictionaries and usage guides.

phosphorus   an element used in matches and fertilizer, among other things. The adjective, *phosporous*, is often misused for the noun—*phosphorus*.

picnic   *picnicked, picnicking, picnicker*.

pig, hog   In its literal sense, a *pig* is defined as a domesticated swine that weighs less than 120 pounds, at which weight it becomes a *hog*.

pitcher   *Pitcher* may be used to refer to a container for liquid or a baseball player but it has nothing to do with art or photography. That word is *picture*.

plan on   *Plan on* followed by a gerund (I *plan on going* home next week.) is widely used but is considered informal. *Plan to* should be used in formal contexts. (I *plan to* go home next week.)

She admired the picture of the pitcher.

playwright   *Playwrights* are people who write plays. Do not call them *playwrites*.

plenty   *Plenty* is in good standing as a noun (There is *plenty of* beer for the party.), but it runs into trouble as an attributive adjective (*plenty* beer). As an adverb (*plenty* cold), it's informal at best.

plurality   See MAJORITY, PLURALITY.

plus   When *plus* joins two noun phrases, the verb takes its number from the main subject, according to most usage guides. (Joan's talent *plus* Jack's money makes the company a success. Four big contracts *plus* a tax break mean a big year.)

p.m   See A.M., P.M.

podium   See LECTERN, PODIUM, DAIS.

poetic justice   an outcome in which just deserts come in an ironically appropriate manner; for example, a serial bomber is killed when a device goes off prematurely.

poetic license   a poet, writer, or artist's deviation from fact or conventional rules, style, or form to achieve a desired effect.

poinsettia   sometimes misspelled.

point-blank   so close to the target that a weapon may be aimed directly at it without considering the drop in the projectile's course (*point-blank* range). The hyphen is preferred, although *pointblank* is not wrong. It also means straightforward, direct, plain, blunt (a *point-blank* answer).

point in time   a bureaucrat's synonym for now or at this (or that) time. It enjoyed popularity during the Senate Watergate hearings in 1973.

politic   now used for *political* only in the phrase *body politic*. *Politic* means prudent, diplomatic, expedient, shrewd, and it is seldom used. (Their decision was *politic*. He took a *politic* stance.)

politicking   Notice the *k*. It means engaging in political discussion or activities. The present tense is *politic* or *politick*. *Politicking* is the present participle. The past tense and past participle are *politicked*. (We were warned about *politicking* too close to the polls.)

politics   singular when referring to the art (*Politics* is a science to them.) and plural when referring to practices. (*Politics* are believed to be the reason the consultant got the job.) See -ICS.

population, populace, populous   *Population* is the total number of people living in a specific area, such as a country, state, or city. (The *popu-*

lation of the United States continues to grow.) *Populace* refers to the common people, the masses, as distinguished from the higher classes, (The *populace* grew more disenchanted.) *Populous* means heavily populated (the city's *populous* east side).

pore, pour   *Pore* means to read or study carefully: "*pore* over old newspapers." *Pour* is often used incorrectly for *pore* ("*poured* over a history book").

port, harbor   Although these two words are used interchangeably, you may wish to observe this distinction: A *harbor* is a shelter for ships, and a *port* is a harbor viewed especially with reference to its commercial activities and facilities. "It's the busiest *port* city on the coast, and it has a fine *harbor.*"

port, starboard, larboard   *Port* is the left side of a ship as you face forward, toward the bow. *Starboard* is the right side. *Larboard* once performed the function of *port*. *Port* became the word of choice, it is said, because of difficulty in distinguishing *larboard* from *starboard* in shouted orders.

Portuguese   The spelling is the same for noun, adjective, plural, and singular, whether you're talking about one Portuguese or twenty Portuguese.

possessed   When *possessed* means owning or having, the preposition is *of* (*possessed of* great wealth). When it means under the control of or dominated by, it takes *by* or *with* (*possessed by* the devil, *possessed by* an idea, *possessed with* a desire for success).

possibility   usually takes the preposition *of*. (Let's investigate the *possibility of* reopening negotiations.)

possible, probable   *Possible* is what may or can exist or come about. *Probable* is something that very likely or with great certainty may exist or happen. (Rain is *possible* today. We will *probably* land the contract.) See FEASIBLE, POSSIBLE. See APT, LIABLE, LIKELY, and LIKELY.

possum, opossum   *Possum* is considered a variant of *opossum*, but the idiom is still *play possum*, which means pretending to be asleep or dead.

postal card, postcard   These two terms are used interchangeably, but technically, a *postal card* is a card issued by the post office with a stamp printed on it and a *postcard* is a card, often with a picture on it, purchased in a commercial establishment such as a drugstore or gift shop. The latter term is sometimes used as two words—*post card*.

postpone   See DELAY, POSTPONE.

potato   Its plural is spelled *potatoes*.

pour   See PORE, POUR.

practicable, practical   *Practicable* means something can be done. *Practical* means it can be done sensibly and usefully. Crossing the street is *practicable* (it can be done), but it's *practical* to cross the street at a traffic signal (the sensible way to do it).

practically, virtually   These two words are used interchangeably in the sense of almost or nearly. But only *practically* can mean "in practice" or "in a practical manner." (We approached the problem *practically*.) *Virtually* is confined to almost, as good as, or in effect. (Our supplies are *virtually* exhausted.)

precede   See PROCEED, PRECEDE.

precedence, precedent   *Precedence* is the act or right of preceding, priority in rank, order or importance. (A general has *precedence* over a colonel.) *Precedent* is an act or instance that may be used as an example or justification for subsequent similar cases, especially legal decisions. (The court's ruling set a *precedent*.) *Precedent* also refers to established practice or custom (break *precedent*).

precipitate, precipitous   The adjective *precipitate* applies to human actions that are hasty, rash, impulsive. (Don't make a *precipitate* decision.) *Precipitous* refers to physical steepness (a *precipitous* slope).

preclude   Its principal preposition is *from*. (A previous commitment *precluded* me *from* attending the meeting.)

predominant, predominate   *Predominant* is preferred for the adjective and *predominate* for the verb. (Red is the *predominant* color. Smith *pre-*

dominated in the final match.) *Predominantly* is the preferred adverb (a *predominantly* blue-collar neighborhood).

preface   The noun is usually followed by *to* (the *preface to* the book) and the verb by *with* (*prefaced* her statement *with* a brief history of the project) and sometimes *by* (a chapter *prefaced by* a brief explanation).

prefer   *Prefer* is usually followed by *to* or *over*. (I *prefer* vodka *to* gin. I *prefer* vodka *over* gin.) However, when *prefer* is followed by an infinitive, use *rather than* and a second infinitive. (I *prefer* to fly *rather than* to drive.) Or you could change the infinitives to participles. (I *prefer* flying to driving.)

prejudicial   most often uses preposition *to* (evidence *prejudicial to* the defendant).

premature   See IMMATURE, PREMATURE.

premiere   use of *premiere* as a verb is unacceptable to a number of usage commentators but is treated as standard by most current desk dictionaries. (The show will *premiere* Friday.)

premise, premises   A *premise* is a proposition on which an argument or reasoning is based. *Premises*, always plural, refers to land and/or buildings on it. (The argument's basic *premise* was faulty. These *premises* are closed to the public.)

preoccupied   usually followed by the preposition *with*. (I was *preoccupied with* my grades.) and sometimes *by*. (He was *preoccupied by* the tragedy of her situation.)

preparatory to   This idiom means *in preparation for*. It refers to one action that leads to a second, and it is not a synonym for *before*. (We packed our bags *preparatory to* flying to London.)

prerequisite   See PERQUISITE, PREREQUISITE.

prescribe, proscribe   To *prescribe* is to order, dictate, direct, require, or recommend something—the use of medicine or treatment, for example. (The doctor *prescribed* [ordered] aspirin and bed rest. My boss *prescribed* [recommended] a brief computer course.) To *proscribe* is to prohibit, outlaw, denounce, condemn, forbid. (The company *proscribed* [outlawed] wild parties in the workplace.)

present   The verb *present* is usually followed by the prepositions *to* (the recipient) or *with* (what is being presented). (We *presented* a check *to* the foundation. We *presented* the foundation *with* a check.) Watch the pronunciation and hyphenation: *pre-sent* for the verb, *pres-ent* for the noun.

present time   *At the present time* is redundant. You can shorten it to *at the present, at present*, or *now*.

presently   Many usage authorities would prefer that use of this word be restricted to soon or shortly. However, it is frequently used to mean now, and this usage is accepted by most recent dictionaries. Usually there is no conflict, because the tense makes the intended meaning clear. (John is *presently* [now] engaged in an affair with Louise. They will come along *presently* [soon].)

preside   Its principal preposition is *over* (Jones *presided over* the meeting.), though *at* is sometimes used. (I *presided at* the bar.) *At* also is used in reference to a featured instrumental performer. (Smith *presided at* the piano.)

presume   See ASSUME, PRESUME.

presumptive, presumptuous   *Presumptive*, meaning based on probability or presumption, is used mainly in a legal sense (*presumptive* evidence, *presumptive* heir). Sometimes it is erroneously used for *presumptuous*, which means bold, forward, arrogant, taking too much for granted. (It was *presumptuous* of the Smiths to join our table uninvited.) See HEIR APPARENT, HEIR PRESUMPTIVE and ASSUME, PRESUME.

pretty   acceptable as an adverb meaning somewhat, fairly, moderately. (She is a *pretty* good sales representative. I'm *pretty* sure.)

prevail   When it means to persuade or induce, *prevail* is most often followed by *on* or *upon* (*prevailed on* them to sing an encore). When the meaning is to gain the advantage of, triumph, the preposition is usually *over* or *against* (*prevailed over* his opponent, *prevailed against* lopsided odds).

prevent, hinder   To *prevent* something is to stop it, to keep it from happening. (Illness *prevented* her from making the speech.) To *hinder* is to get in the way of, obstruct, or delay the progress of something. (The murder of two key witnesses *hindered* the investigation.) See HINDER.

preventive, preventative   The shorter form is preferred (*preventive* maintenance, *preventive* medicine).

principal, principle   *Principal* as an adjective means chief or foremost and as a noun means chief person or leader. (He played the *principal* character. John was a *principal* in Joan's divorce suit. He is the high school *principal*.) A *principle* is a rule of action or conduct or a doctrine or tenet (a person of high *principles*, a *principle* of physics).

prior to   Usage commentators score *prior to* as a stilted term found in places where *before* would be more appropriate, but dictionaries do not join in this rejection. (*Prior to* becoming the hotel's chef, Joan was a short-order cook at a greasy spoon.)

probation   See PARDON, PAROLE, PROBATION.

proceed, precede   *Proceed* means to go forward or onward, especially after a pause. (We *proceeded* to the next item on the agenda. We stopped for gas, then *proceeded* on to the ball park.) It should not be used for go, come, travel, walk, move, as in "They *proceeded* to the bar." Don't use it in wordy expressions such as "I *proceeded* to open the meeting," meaning "I opened the meeting." *Proceed* is sometimes confused with *precede,* which means to go before. (Five aides *preceded* the general into the meeting. Jack was *preceded* in the position by one of the brightest people in the business.)

prodigal   recklessly wasteful. Some folks, remembering the parable about the son who received his share of his father's goods and squandered it with riotous living in "a far country," think *prodigal* means wandering. But the meaning has to do with the squandering, not the traveling.

proficient   most often followed by the prepositions *in* and *at*. (She was *proficient in* French. He was *proficient at* his job.)

profit   Usually followed by the prepositions *from* or *by* (I *profited from* my investment; I *profited by* the experience).

progress Watch the pronunciation and hyphenation. As a verb, it's pronounced *pro-GRESS* and hyphenated the same way. As a noun, it's *PROG-ress* and the hyphenation changes accordingly.

prohibit Most often followed by *from*. ("They *prohibited* us *from* entering the hall.") *Prohibit to* is rarely used.

project As a noun, it's hyphenated and pronounced PROJ-ect. As a verb, it's pro-JECT.

Cyril lay prostrate before the king.

prone, supine, prostrate In strict usage, *prone* and *prostrate* mean in a flat position, face down; *supine* means to lie flat, face up. *Prone* and *prostrate* are now used for a horizontal position facing either direction. *Supine* is still used only for facing upward. (The troops assumed a *prone* position to perform pushups. The exhausted runner crossed the finish line and fell *prostrate*. He was *supine* on the grass, watching the fluffy clouds.) *Prostrate* is sometimes misused in references to the *prostate gland*.

pronunciation often mispronounced *pronounciation* and misspelled the same way.

propellant, propellent *Propellant* is the preferred spelling as a noun, though *propellent* is not incorrect. Both are acceptable as an adjective but here *propellent* is the more popular choice.

prophecy, prophesy A *prophecy* (PROF-uh-see, a noun) is a prediction, a revelation of what is to come. (The *prophecy* was one of gloom and doom.) To *prophesy* (PROF-uh-sigh, a verb), is to foretell, to predict. (The stock market analyst *prophesied* a quick recovery.)

propitious Takes prepositions *for* and *to*. (I found a *propitious* location for starting my business. The day was *propitious for* our arrival. The time was *propitious to* visit the lawyer. The offer seemed *propitious to* our side.)

proscribe See PRESCRIBE, PROSCRIBE.

prosecute   See PERSECUTE, PROSECUTE.

prostrate   See PRONE, SUPINE, PROSTRATE.

protagonist   A *protagonist* is the principal character in a literary work, and, by extension, the leading figure in a real event. For instance, Hamlet was the *protagonist* in Shakespeare's play and Henry Kissinger was the *protagonist* in Middle East peace efforts while he was American secretary of state. Dictionaries accept the use of *protagonist* for advocate, champion, proponent, although most usage commentators object.

prototype   A *prototype* is the first of its kind, an original or model on which something is formed or based, a pattern, an archetype, such as the trial model of an aircraft under development.

proved, proven   Both are correct as the past participle of *prove*, but *proved* is preferred in most cases. (They have *proved* their point.) *Proven* is more commonly used as an adjective directly before a noun (a *proven* talent).

provide   uses prepositions *for, to*, and *with* (*providing for* the poor, *providing* jobs *for* students, *providing* aid *to* schools, *providing* workers *with* raises).

provided, providing   These two words are interchangeable, but *provided* is more commonly used and there is a preference for it among most critics and some dictionaries. (You may leave at noon *provided* [or *providing*] you have finished your work.)

psychedelic   Refers to a mental state characterized by hallucinations or intensified awareness and sensory perceptions brought on by drugs such as LSD. Often misspelled *psychodelic*.

punish   takes the prepositions *for, by*, and *with* (*punished for* skipping school, *punished by* spanking, *punished with* a whip).

pupil, student   *Pupil* usually refers to someone in the elementary grades and *student* to someone in high school or college.

puppet, marionette   Both of these words apply to a small figure of an animal or person with jointed limbs manipulated from above by strings or wires. Only *puppet* is used in the extended sense—a person, group, or government whose actions are controlled by others (a *puppet* government, a *puppet* of the coup leader).

purge   followed most often by *of* (*purged* the party *of* dissidents) and sometimes *from*. (Less desirable subjects were *purged from* the curriculum.)

purport   to give the appearance, to profess. Some critics discourage its use in the passive voice. They also say the subject may not be a person as such, but I find examples of this in recent dictionaries (a person *purporting* to be a journalist).

purposefully, purposely   *Purposefully* means resolutely, in a determined manner. (They worked *purposefully* to complete the project on schedule.) *Purposely* means intentionally, on purpose, deliberately. (They *purposely* missed the meeting. He made the remark *purposely* to annoy me.)

pursuit Its preposition is *of* (*pursuit of* happiness, in *pursuit of* answers).

pyjamas See PAJAMAS, PYJAMAS.

Q

quaint, queer   *Quaint* is charmingly curious in a pleasing, old-fashioned way (a *quaint* cottage). *Queer* is strange, odd, eccentric, shady, suspicious (something *queer* about the plans for the development).

quandary   sometimes misspelled *quandry*.

query   *Query* is a synonym of *question* and *inquiry,* according to some dictionaries, but usage authorities say it applies to a specific, limited matter. (I received a *query* from the IRS about certain deductions.) It should not be used as a synonym for *inquiry* or *question* in a sense of investigation or interrogation. (The coroner's *inquiry* lasted two weeks. The committee bombarded the job applicant with *questions*.)

questionnaire   not *questionaire*.

queue   See CUE, QUEUE.

quick, quickly   *Quick* is acceptable as an adverb, but *quickly* is preferred in formal prose and speech. *Quick* usually appears in brief remarks such as "Come *quick*! Junior just wrecked the tricycle."

quieten   a verb synonymous with *quiet* that is in use in Britain but is heard only occasionally in the United States. Often followed by *down*. Most dictionaries list it but don't give it a label except to indicate that it is a Briticism.

R

rabbit, rarebit   See WELSH RABBIT, RAREBIT.

raccoon   double *c*.

She racked her brain
trying to find the answer.

rack, wrack   *Rack* means to torture, strain or stretch, and *wrack* means destruction, wreckage, to wreck or be wrecked (*racked* one's brains, *nerve-racking*, *racked* with pain, *storm-wracked*, *wrack* and ruin). However, dictionaries are listing the two terms as variants of one another, so sometimes you see "*nerve-wracking*" and "*rack and ruin*." See NERVE-RACKING.

racket, racquet   *Racket* is the preferred spelling.

raise   See RISE, RAISE.

raise, rear   Both of these words are used for people and animals in the sense of bringing them up.

rarefy   To make thin or less dense, as a gas (*rarefied* mountain air). Figuratively, to purify, make more refined (the *rarefied* atmosphere at the gathering of campus intellectuals). It is often misspelled *rarify*.

rarely ever   a redundancy. Make it *rarely*. "Rarely, if ever," is acceptable.

rather   *Had rather* is correct usage, but *would rather* is more common. (I *would rather* [*had rather*] stay home.)

rational, rationale   *Rational* means based on or exercising reason, sane, lucid, logical, sensible. (He made a *rational* decision. The patient was *rational*.) *Rationale* means the fundamental reason or logical basis. (I see the *rationale* behind the plan.)

ravage, ravish   To *ravage* is to create great destruction, devastate. (The raiders *ravaged* the village. The storm *ravaged* the downtown area.) To *rav-*

ish is to carry off by force, rape. (The raiders *ravished* the women.) It also means to overwhelm with joy or delight, enrapture. *Ravishing* is entrancing, unusually attractive, pleasing, or striking.

ravel, unravel *Ravel* means to tangle as well as to disentangle. *Unravel* shares the untangling sense, and in addition means to make clear or solve, as a mystery.

real, really The use of *real* in place of *really* as an adverb meaning *very* is labeled informal or colloquial in current dictionaries (*real* tired, *real* fast). Though it is often heard in conversation, it should be shunned in favor of *really* in serious speech or writing. (They're *really* good at this.)

rear See RAISE, REAR.

reason is because Even though *the reason is because* is in common use, it is discouraged by most usage guides and dictionaries, which recommend *the reason is that*. (The *reason* I am late *is that* I had a flat tire.)

rebellion, revolution A *rebellion* is open, armed, organized resistance to government that usually fails. A *revolution* is the overthrow by force of a government and its replacement with another (the Whiskey *Rebellion*, the American *Revolution*).

receptive usually followed by the preposition *to* (*receptive to* new ideas).

reckon *Reckon* is to count, figure up, compute, calculate (I *reckon* we lost $100,000.) and to consider, regard as. (I *reckon* her to be an authority.) It is considered dialectal when used to mean think or suppose. (I *reckon* they'll be late.)

reconcile uses prepositions *to* and *with*. (He was *reconciled to* frequent trips. *Reconcile* my ideas *with* yours.)

reconnaissance frequently misspelled.

record Surpassing all others, as in performance, size, amount. *New record* is usually incorrect unless previous records are involved in the discussion. The verb is hyphenated re-cord and pronounced re-CORD, and the noun hyphenated rec-ord and pronounced RECK-ord.

recourse, resort, resource   *Resource* is a source of support or supply available when it is needed. *Recourse* and *resort* both refer to turning to a person or thing for help or protection. *Resort* has more of a sense of finality than *recourse*, as in "last resort." (We had hidden *resources*. I sought *recourse* in the courts.)

recreation, re-creation   *Recreation* is the refreshment of your mind and body, perhaps after work, with some sort of pastime or pleasant exercise. (My favorite *recreation* was shooting baskets in the backyard.) The hyphen is essential in *re-creation*, creating anew. (They hoped the investigation would provide a *re-creation* of the events that led up to the crime.)

recrimination, accusation   *Recrimination* is a countercharge against one's accuser. (Smith's accusation brought swift *recrimination* from Jones.)

recur, reoccur   *Recur* is preferred, as is *recurrence*. *Reoccur* has nearly vanished.

recuse   a term infrequently seen and confined mostly to court cases. When a judge decides to withdraw from hearing a case because of a prejudice or conflict of interest, he or she *recuses* himself or herself.

redolent   odorous or smelling strongly and suggestive or reminiscent. Its principal preposition is *of* (a kitchen *redolent of* garlic, a town *redolent of* the frontier days).

refer   See ALLUDE, REFER.

referendum   plural: *referendums* preferred to *referenda*.

reflective, reflexive   Although *reflective* may be used in senses related to *reflection*, its chief use is as a synonym for *meditative, pensive*. (I found her in a *reflective* mood.) *Reflexive* is used almost solely in a grammatical sense, applied to a verb having the same thing or person for its subject and direct object, as *injured* in "I *injured* myself," and to a pronoun used in such a construction (*myself* in the example).

refute   to prove a statement or accusation is false, according to most usage guides and dictionaries. (We presented the auditor's report to *refute* the allegation that the treasurer had mishandled the organization's funds.)

Refute is often used when proof is absent, when a better word might be deny, dispute, rebut, or reject.

regard   The phrases *as regards*, *in regard to*, and *with regard to* are all standard English. *In regards to* and *with regards to* are not.

regardless   ordinarily should be followed by the preposition *of*. It means in spite of, without regard for (*regardless of* the risk, *regardless of* political affiliation).

regretful, regrettable   *Regretful*—filled with regret or sorrow—is sometimes used erroneously for *regrettable*, which means causing or deserving regret, unfortunate. (The cancellation of the game was *regrettable*. The people holding tickets to the game were *regretful* when it was rained out.)

reign, rein   *Reign* means to rule, to govern. (The coup ended the king's 25-year *reign*.) *Reins* are bridle straps that control a horse. The verb *rein* used literally and figuratively means to restrain, control. (The chief *reined* in the overzealous traffic officers. The Joneses kept their teenager under tight *rein*.) *Rein* and *reign* are often misused for one another.

reiterate   See ITERATE, REITERATE.

relation, relative   These terms are interchangeable as nouns applying to kin, but there is a slight preference for *relative*. It's *relation/relative of*, not *to*, but it's *related to*.

relevant   Pertinent to the matter under discussion, usually followed by *to*. What something is relevant to is ordinarily explained. (That testimony was *relevant to* another case.)

relish   The noun is most often followed by *for* (her *relish for* opera). *Of* is also acceptable.

reluctant, reticent   *Reluctant* is unwilling, disinclined (*reluctant* to make a change). *Reticent* is disposed to be silent, reserved, uncommunicative. (We were able to learn little from her *reticent* friend.) *Reluctant* usually refers to action, *reticent* to speech.

remand   to send back. In legal usage, *remand* is to return a prisoner to custody during further investigation or proceedings. (The prisoner was *remanded* to the county jail.) or to return a case to a lower court with instructions for additional action. (The case was *remanded to* district court for resentencing.) The phrase *remand back* is redundant.

remedial, remediable   *Remedial* describes something that is intended to serve as a remedy (*remedial* reading). *Remediable* is something that is capable of being remedied (a *remediable* problem).

remind   to cause to remember, to put in mind of something. It must take an object. (The meeting will be held Friday, the pastor *reminded* the congregation. Wrong: The meeting will be held Friday, the pastor *reminded*.)

renown   This is a noun (a city of great *renown*). Do not use *renown* as an adjective. The adjective is *renowned* (a *renowned* authority on jungle rot). It's sometimes misspelled *reknown*.

reoccur   See RECUR, REOCCUR.

repertoire, repertory   Both terms apply to the plays, songs, and such that an actor or theatrical group is prepared to perform, although *repertoire* is preferred in this sense. (It didn't take long for the group to exhaust its *repertoire*.) *Repertory* alone describes a company that produces and performs several works during a season (*repertory* theater), and it alone refers to the store or stock of such a company.

replace   See SUBSTITUTE, REPLACE.

replete   abundantly full, plentifully supplied, a sense of overflowing not conveyed by complete or furnished with. Its preposition is *with*. (They set out a table *replete with* all our favorite foods.)

replica   In its strictest sense, in arts circles, a *replica* is a reproduction of a work of art made by or under the supervision of the original artist. (Some preferred the artist's *replica* to the original.) In a broader sense, it is applied to any close copy or reproduction (a *replica* of the *Santa Maria*).

reprisal   usually used with *against* (a perpetrator) and *for* (an action). (The vandalism was a *reprisal against* the council *for* enacting the curfew.)

resemblance   followed most often by the preposition *to* (bears a strong *resemblance to* his father) and in some cases *between*. (We found little *resemblance between* the two proposals.)

resort   See RECOURSE, RESORT, RESOURCE.

resource   See RECOURSE, RESORT, RESOURCE.

Even as a baby, he bore a strong resemblance to his father.

restaurateur   frequently misspelled *restauranteur*.

restive, restless   Both of these words mean unquiet, incapable of resting or relaxing, but *restive* alone means impatient under restrictions or delay. (The horse was *restless* in the pasture. The horse grew *restive* when it was tied to the pole.)

retch, wretch   To *retch* is to attempt to vomit. A *wretch* is a miserable, unfortunate person or a vile, despicable person.

reticent See RELUCTANT, RETICENT.

revel   Its main preposition is *in* (*reveling in* their victory).

revert   to go back to a previous state, practice, position, etc. *Revert back* is usually redundant.

review, revue   A *revue* is a theatrical production of satirical songs, skits, and dances, the word's only meaning. Although this also is one of the many definitions of *review,* the preference for this sense is *revue*.

revolution   See REBELLION, REVOLUTION.

revolve around   See CENTER AROUND.

revue   See REVIEW, REVUE.

rhetoric   Its primary meaning is the art of effective and persuasive use of language in speech and writing. (The senator's *rhetoric* held the crowd spellbound.) It also is sometimes used to describe artificial eloquence. Its use in a pejorative sense is usually preceded by an attribute (mere *rhetoric*, empty *rhetoric*, flimsy *rhetoric*, political *rhetoric*).

rhinoceros   The plural is *rhinoceroses* (a slight preference) or *rhinoceros*, or (rarely) *rhinoceri*.

rich   Its principal preposition is *in* (*rich in* natural resources) and it is used less frequently with *with* (a dessert *rich with* chocolate).

rid   most often used with *of*. (I *rid* my house *of* mice. They were glad to be *rid of* us. We got *rid of* a bunch of junk.)

right   widely used as an adverb meaning *very, extremely*, but it is considered informal or colloquial in this sense. (I was *right* glad to see him. We had a *right* pleasant day.)

ring, rang, rung   *Rang* is the preferred past tense; *rung* is the past participle.

rise, raise   The verb *raise* is always transitive. (I *raised* my hand.) *Rise* is always intransitive. (The crowd *rose* to cheer.) As a noun, *raise* is used instead of *rise* for a salary increase and an increase in a bet.

rob   Its preposition is *of*. (They *robbed* me *of* twenty dollars. The people *robbed* them *of* their dignity.)

robbery   See BURGLARY, ROBBERY, THEFT.

rock 'n' roll   *Rock 'n' roll* is the preferred construction.

round, around   These two words are used interchangeably, but *round* is the preference in such expressions as *all-round, round-the-clock, year-round*, and *round the world*.

S

sacrilegious Apparently because this word deals with disrepect and irreverence toward something that is sacred, some people connect it with *religion* and spell it *sacreligious*. It is the adjective of *sacrilege*. Adding to the confusion, the preferred pronunciation in most dictionaries is *sack-ra-lidg-us*, as in *religious*.

Sahara You see many references to the *Sahara desert*, even though *Sahara* comes from an Arabic word meaning *desert*; therefore, *desert* is redundant. You'd be more accurate to say simply *Sahara* or, perhaps even better, *the Sahara*.

St. James See COURT OF ST. JAMES'S.

salmonella a bacteria that causes food poisoning. Its name doesn't come from fish, but rather Daniel E. Salmon, an American pathologist. It's pronounced *SAL-muh-NELL-uh*.

sanatorium, sanitarium The distinction between these two words has blurred, and both are now applied to an institution involved in the treatment of chronic diseases, such as tuberculosis, or for rest and recuperation, a health resort.

sang See SING, SANG, SUNG.

sank See SINK, SANK, SUNK, SUNKEN.

saturate Its principal preposition is *with* (water *saturated with* chlorine, a speech *saturated with* anecdotes).

save *Save* used as a preposition in the sense of *except* or *but* is criticized by usage commentators, but most dictionaries present it without a label. (Everyone has left *save* Jane and Harry.) See EXCEPT.

scan This word has two completely different meanings: to examine thoroughly, and to glance at hastily, both standard in American usage. Be certain the context makes clear which sense you are using. (We *scanned* the report carefully. I *scanned* the sports section quickly.)

scarcely   A clause following *scarcely* should be introduced by *when* or *before*, not *than*. (I *scarcely* got inside *when* [not than] the phone rang.) And *scarcely* is a negative, so don't use it with another negative. Avoid "couldn't *scarcely*, without *scarcely*, etc. See HARDLY and SOONER.

Scot, Scottish, Scotch   Use *Scot, Scotsman*, or *Scotswoman* to refer to the people of Scotland (Mary Queen of *Scots*). Usage guides and dictionaries say *Scotchman* and *Scotchwoman* are considered mildly offensive and should be avoided. The proper adjectives are *Scottish* and *Scots* (*Scottish* rite, *Scots* Guards). *Scotch* is used for things, such as *Scotch* whisky, *Scotch* broth, *Scotch* plaid. See BRITON, BRITISHER, ENGLISHMAN.

scrip, script   *Scrip* is paper money issued for temporary use in emergency situations. (The employees were paid in *scrip* during the financial crisis.) *Script* is handwriting or the text of a play, movie, or television or radio broadcast.

sculpt   A back-formation that is accepted as a synonym of the verb form of *sculpture* (*sculpted* a statue).

search   The noun *search* is usually followed by the preposition *for* except in the phrase *in search of* (the *search for* gold, in *search of* truth).

seasonable, seasonal   *Seasonable* is appropriate for the season (July Fourth will be *seasonably* warm.), occurring at the right time, opportune, timely. (The offer of help came at a *seasonable* time.) *Seasonal* applies to something dependent on or controlled by the seasons (*seasonal* employment, *seasonal* increase in toy sales).

secure   Usage guides discourage the use of *secure* as a synonym of *get*, as in "We stopped in the village to *secure* some groceries." The suggested sense is to *obtain* something with certainty after great effort and retain it. (The defendant *secured* the best defense attorney in the state.)

self-destruct   See DESTRUCT, SELF-DESTRUCT.

semimonthly   See BIMONTHLY, SEMIMONTHLY.

semiweekly   See BIWEEKLY, SEMIWEEKLY.

sensual, sensuous   *Sensual* applies to gratification of the physical senses (*sensual* excesses, *sensual* pleasures); *sensuous* refers to the senses involved in the aesthetic enjoyment of music, art, etc. (*sensuous* poetry, *sensuous* music). *Sensual* also carries overtones of grossness or lewdness not found in *sensuous*.

serve, service   To *service* is to provide maintenance for, to repair. Do not use for *serve* in the sense of providing goods or services. (The station *serviced* [not served] my car. The power company *serves* [not services] three states.)

sct, sit   *Set*, usually a transitive verb, means to place or put. (*Set* the plate on the table.) There are exceptions. (The sun *sets*. The hen *sets* on her eggs—though *sit* is also used here.) *Sit* is usually intransitive and means "place oneself." (They *sat* on chairs in the small room.) Exception: "The waiter *sat* us next to the window."

Imogene sits down at the table even though a place has not been set for her.

sewage, sewerage   These two words have become interchangeable for wastewater, but only *sewerage* is used for the system of sewers used to dispose of the waste.

shan't   standard as a contraction of *shall not*. It is more common in Great Britain than in the United States.

sherbet   This spelling is preferred to *sherbert*, which is generally considered incorrect.

shined, shone   *Shone* is the preferred past tense and participle of *shine* except in the sense of polishing (shoes, metal, etc.), where *shined* is most often used. (The stars *shone* brightly. I *shined* the doorknobs.)

ship   See BOAT, SHIP.

short shrift   *Short shrift* is a brief time granted a condemned prisoner for confession and absolution before his execution. It also means little care or attention in dealing with something. To make *short shrift of* is to make short work of a matter, to dispose of it quickly and impatiently. (The store manager made *short shrift of* my complaint.)

should of   an unacceptable term sometimes used because it sounds like *should've* (*should have*), the intended construction. For this reason, you also frequently see *could of* and *would of*.

showed, shown   The past tense of *show* is *showed*. The past participle is *showed* or *shown*, with *shown* found more often. (The usher *showed* me to my seat. They have *shown* their expertise.)

shrink   *Shrank* or *shrunk* for past tense, with *shrank* slightly preferred. *Shrunk* or *shrunken* for past participle, with *shrunk* usually used when the participle performs as a verb and *shrunken* when it is used as an adjective. (I *shrank* my shirts. My shirts *shrank*. My shirts have *shrunk*. I threw away my *shrunken* shirts.)

sick to/at one's stomach   Either is acceptable, with *to* a bit of a favorite.

sight, site, cite   These sound-alikes are often confused (a *site* for sore eyes [should be *sight*], a construction *sight* [*site*], they *sited* the record [*cited*]). *Cite* is not ordinarily used for the others.

sightseer   also *sightsee* and *sightseeing*.

simplistic   This means *oversimplified* and should not be used for *simple*. It is usually used in a disparaging sense. (The proposed solution was dismissed as *simplistic*.)

simultaneous   not to be used as an adverb, as in "The award ceremony was held *simultaneous* with his birthday." The adverb is *simultaneously*.

since   See AGO, SINCE.

sing, sang, sung   *Sung* occasionally appears as the past tense of *sing*, and not incorrectly, but *sang* is the predominant form. *Sung* is the past participle.

sink, sank, sunk, sunken   The past tense may be *sank* or *sunk*. *Sank* is preferred (*sank* the ship). *Sunk* is the past participle. (We have *sunk* the ship.) *Sunken* is used only as an adjective, usually attributively (*sunken* treasure).

sit   See SET, SIT.

site   See SIGHT, SITE, CITE.

sizable   not *sizeable*.

ski   *skis, skied, skiing, skier*.

slander   See LIBEL, SLANDER.

slave   takes the prepositions *to* and *of* (a *slave to* duty, the *slave of* a manipulating child).

slay   Its past tense is *slew* (The knight *slew* five dragons.), but *slayed* is used in the show business sense of delight or amuse immensely. (The skit *slayed* 'em.)

slow, slowly   Both of these words are acceptable as adverbs. *Slow* is often found in compounds such as *slow-moving, slow-talking*, and *slow-burning*. It is also used in idiomatic expressions such as "go *slow*" or "drive *slow*," although *slowly* would not be incorrect in these cases and in formal writing would be preferred.

Smithsonian Institution   not *Smithsonian Institute*.

smolder   preferred to *smoulder*, which is the British choice.

sneak, snuck   *Snuck* is frequently used as past tense and past participle of *sneak* to portray regional dialogue or to achieve a breezy effect in speech and informal writing. (We *snuck* around the corner and surprised the sleeping handyman.) Its use in more serious efforts is discouraged by usage commentators and most dictionaries.

so-called   commonly or incorrectly called (*so-called* think tank, *so-called* friends). Do not put quotation marks around the noun preceded by *so-called*. Wrong: abandoned by his *so-called* "friends."

solicitous   anxious, showing concern. It is usually followed by the prepositions *about, for,* and *of* (*solicitous of* my well-being, *solicitous about* their future, *solicitous for* my health).

someplace   *Somewhere* is preferred, although *someplace* is frequently used, usually in an informal sense.

sometime, some time   *Sometime* is one word when used as an adverb meaning at an indefinite time. (Let's get together *sometime*.) It's *some time*, two words, when *some* becomes an adjective modifying the noun *time* to form a phrase meaning an unspecified interval or period of time. (This has been going on for *some time*.)

sooner   The phrase *no sooner* should be followed by *than* rather than *when*. (I had *no sooner* answered the telephone *than* [not when] the doorbell rang.)

sparing   takes the prepositions *in* and *of* (*sparing in* their praise, *sparing of* encouragement).

spay   Its past tense is *spayed*. It sometimes appears incorrectly as *spade* or *spaded*.

special   See ESPECIAL, SPECIAL.

spelled, spelt   *Spelt* is a variant past tense and past participle of *spell*. It is rarely used in the United States but is fairly common in Great Britain.

spilled, spilt   The variant past tense and past participle *spilt* is preferred in British English but is hardly ever used in American English except sometimes idiomatically as an adjective (*spilt* milk).

spiral   can be up or down. It most commonly applies to a continuous increase or decrease in wages, prices, etc. (the *spiral* of increasing wages and prices).

spit   Either *spit* or *spat* is correct as the past tense and past participle of *spit*. The British prefer *spat*; *spit* seems to be more common in American English.

spitting image   This form is slightly more common than *spit and image*. Both are acceptable (the *spitting image* of his father).

spoonful   The plural is *spoonfuls*. Also, *tablespoonfuls, teaspoonfuls*, etc. *Spoonsful* is rarely used. See −FUL.

stadium   Its plurals are *stadiums* and *stadia*. *Stadiums* is preferred for modern facilities, and *stadia* for the older senses closer to the word's Greek origins, such as the ancient courses for foot races and the unit of length.

staffer   This term for a member of a staff enjoys acceptance by nearly all recent dictionaries (a newspaper *staffer*).

stalactite, stalagmite   Both are deposits of calcium carbonate formed by water dripping in a cave. A *stalactite* hangs from the roof like an icicle; a *stalagmite* builds up from the floor.

stanch, staunch   These words are interchangeable, but *stanch* is used more often as a verb meaning to check or halt the flow of something, such as a liquid, especially blood. (They fashioned a tourniquet to *stanch* the bleeding. Officials were stymied in their attempt to *stanch* the flow of drugs.) *Staunch* appears more often as an adjective meaning firm, steadfast (a *staunch* supporter).

starboard   See PORT, STARBOARD, LARBOARD.

Star-Spangled Banner   See NATIONAL ANTHEM.

stationary, stationery   *Stationary* means having a fixed position, not moving (a *stationary* front). *Stationery* is writing material (written on official *stationery*).

statistics   *Statistics* takes a singular verb when referring to the subject itself. (*Statistics* is my obsession.) Use a plural verb for the data themselves. (These *statistics* prove our point.) See –ICS.

statute, statue   A *statute* is a law, and a *statue* is a three-dimensional likeness, usually of a person. Wrong: "the *Statute* of Liberty" or "*statue* of limitations."

stave   *Staved* and *stove* are both acceptable for the past tense and past participle, with *staved* preferred. *Stove* seems to be confined to nautical contexts. Both use the preposition *in* except in the sense of ward off, which takes *off* (*staved in* four ribs, *staved off* foreclosure). (The bulkhead was *stove in*.)

stink   Past tense is *stank* or *stunk* with *stank* favored. Both are standard. *Stunk* is the past participle. (Our team *stank/stunk* last night. That shed has *stunk* for two weeks.)

straitjacket, strait-laced   These forms are preferred to *straightjacket* and *straight-laced*, which are given as variants by dictionaries. A handful of commentators and one dictionary list *straitlaced* (no hyphen) as their preference.

The socks stank.

stratum, strata   *Strata* is the preferred plural of *stratum*, though *stratums* is accepted. *Strata* as a singular and *stratas* as its plural are not acceptable.

subject   The noun is followed most often by *of* (the *subject of* the book) and sometimes *for* (picked a *subject for* discussion). The adjective and verb are followed by *to* (*subject to* colds, *subjected to* ridicule).

subpoena   *subpoenas, subpoenaed, subpoenaing.*

substitute, replace   *Substitute* means put in place of and takes the preposition *for*. (The chef *substituted* potatoes *for* carrots.) *Replace* means to take the place of and is followed by *with* or *by*. (He *replaced* carrots *with* potatoes. Carrots were *replaced by* potatoes.) In all three examples, you wind up with potatoes.

suffer   *Suffer from* is the heavy preference over *suffer with* when referring to ailments, although *suffer with* is not improper (*suffering from* pneumonia).

suitable   Its principal preposition is *for* (a jacket *suitable for* a cool evening). See ADAPTED, SUITABLE.

suit, suite   *Suit* applies to clothing, cards, or court action (a gray *suit*, follow *suit*, a malpractice *suit*), *suite* to a retinue, music, rooms, or furniture (a ballet *suite*, a hotel *suite*).

sung   See SING, SANG, SUNG.

sunk, sunken   See SINK, SANK, SUNK, SUNKEN.

superior   See INFERIOR, SUPERIOR.

supersede   not *supercede*.

supine   See PRONE, SUPINE, PROSTRATE.

susceptible   Its principal preposition is *to* (*susceptible to* colds).

suspect   The verb is usually followed by *of* (*suspected of* conspiracy). See ACCUSED, SUSPECTED.

swell   Both *swelled* and *swollen* are correct as the past participle of *swell*. *Swollen* is used most often attributively (the *swollen* river) except for the phrase *swelled* head. The past tense is *swelled*.

swim   Its past tense is *swam* (I *swam* across the pond.) and its past participle *swum*. (We had swum there before.)

sympathy   See EMPATHY, SYMPATHY.

T

tactics   Use a singular verb when referring to *tactics* as an art or science. (*Tactics* is taught at the academy.) Use a plural verb in most general references. (The candidate's *tactics* were described as deplorable.) See –ICS.

talesman, talisman   Originally, a *talesman* was a person selected from among those in court or standing nearby to fill a vacancy on a jury that had become deficient in number. Now the term is applied to a member of a regular jury pool or a special pool assembled to provide members for a panel depleted through challenges or for other reasons. A *talisman* is an object believed to be a charm that keeps away evil and brings good fortune.

taps   This is a bugle call that signals lights out for American military personnel. It is not a musical composition; therefore, it is not capitalized (*taps*) and does not require quote marks. It can take either a plural or singular verb, but singular is more commonly used. (The soldiers watched television until *taps* was sounded.) Taps also is blown at military funerals and many memorial services.

tasteful, tasty   *Tasteful* means showing good taste. (Their furniture was *tasteful*.) *Tasty* means savory. (The steak was *tasty*.)

taut ship, tight ship   Either may be used to describe an efficient, well-disciplined operation. They may be applied to a ship or business, institution, etc. (The new CEO runs a *taut ship*.)

teach   See LEARN, TEACH.

temblor   synonym for *earthquake*. It comes from a Spanish word meaning to shake or tremble. *Trembler* and *tremblor* are not accepted.

temperature   The use of *temperature* for fever is recognized as standard in current dictionaries. (I was running a *temperature*. Harriet was in bed with a *temperature*.)

tendency   uses the prepositions *to* and *toward* (a *tendency to* drift, a *tendency toward* tardiness).

tendinitis   This is the preferred spelling, though *tendonitis* is given as a variant by some dictionaries.

tend to   This phrase is used frequently for *pay attention to, attend to*. This use is permitted by most dictionaries and rejected by some critics, who would prefer *attend to* in serious writing. (It was suggested that we *tend to* our own business.)

thankfully   in a thankful manner, gratefully. (The destitute family *thankfully* accepted the food.) It is commonly used to mean fortunately or we/I are thankful that, as in "*Thankfully*, the meeting lasted only an hour," a use that is considered informal by several authorities and not addressed by most dictionaries.

that, adv.   *That* is properly used to mean "to such an extent or degree." (I missed by *that much*.) and "to a high degree, very, extremely," often with a negative. (It's *not that* important.)

that, which   Use *that* to introduce a restrictive clause (one without which the sentence would make no sense), and *which* to introduce a nonrestrictive clause (one the sentence could lose without hurting it). (The book *that* I read last night is on the table. The book, *which* had been on the table, is gone.) The nonrestrictive clause is almost always set off with commas.

theater, theatre   *Theater* is preferred in general use in this country. (This town has three *theaters*.) *Theatre* is British English and is used frequently in proper names: The Tri-County Repertory *Theatre*, Schubert *Theatre*.

thee, thou   *Thee* is an archaic pronoun in the second person objective case meaning *you*. (The warm weather suits *thee*.) *Thou* is the nominative case. (*Thou* will leave tomorrow.)

theft   See BURGLARY, ROBBERY, THEFT.

theism   See DEISM, THEISM.

therefor, therefore   *Therefor* means for that or in return for that. (Helen explained her proposal and her reasoning *therefor*.) *Therefore* means consequently, as a result, hence. (Charlie lost his money and, *therefore*, his seat at the poker table.)

theretofore   until then, before then (a *theretofore* unheard of entertainer).

threshold   not *threshhold*.

thrill   usually followed by the prepositions *to* or *at* (*thrilled at* the thought, *thrilled to* the memory).

thusly   considered a worthless variant of *thus*. Should be confined to attempts to produce a humorous effect.

tight, tightly   As an adverb, *tight* almost always follows the verb it modifies (hold *tight*) and ordinarily is used with such verbs as *squeeze, shut, hold, close*, and *tie* as well as such idioms as *sit tight* and *sleep tight*. *Tightly* may be used in many of the same constructions, but it may also precede the verb (a *tightly* knit group, I clutched it *tightly*).

till, until   *Till* and *until* are interchangeable as both prepositions and conjunctions. Do not use *'til* or *'till*. (We danced *till* dawn. They waited *until* we left.)

tired   usually followed by *of*. (I'm *tired of* this job.)

together with   Usually, when *together with* introduces an addition to a singular subject, the subject remains singular. (The company, *together with* two subsidiaries, was insolvent.) This applies also to in addition to, as well as, along with, besides, and like.

tome   Originally, referred to a volume forming a part of a larger work. It still means this and is also used as a synonym for a book, usually a large, heavy, scholarly one.

tormented   most often followed by the preposition *by* (*tormented by* memories of the accident). Infrequently followed by *with* (*tormented with* anxiety).

tortuous, torturous   *Tortuous* is twisting, winding, and, figuratively, not direct or straightforward (the *tortuous* trail down the mountain, a *tortuous* explanation of their scheme). *Torturous* involves pain, torture. (The boxer received a *torturous* beating.)

toward, towards   *Toward* is the preferred form in American English. *Towards* is the prevailing form in Great Britain.

track, tract   These words are occasionally confused. In "The plan to build houses on the *track* was opposed by its neighbors," the term required is *tract*—a piece of land.

transmute   followed most often by *into* (*transmuted* a slum *into* an urban showpiece) and less often by *to* (*transmuted* lead *to* gold).

transpire   Long used to mean released from secrecy, to become known (A few details have *transpired* from yesterday's closed-door meeting.), *transpire* has now taken on the widely used meaning of to happen, take place, occur. (You won't believe what *transpired* in the courtroom.) Some dictionaries and usage authorities regard this usage as standard but caution that it has many critics who consider it loose or informal.

tread   Its past tense is *trod* and past participle *trod* or *trodden*. (That star has *trod* the boards for 50 years.) The idiom *tread water* takes *treaded* for its past tense and past participle.

trigger   a legitimate verb meaning *initiate, set off,* or *precipitate*. (Wilson's statement to the police *triggered* a series of arrests.)

triumphal, triumphant   *Triumphal* is pertaining to or celebrating or commemorating a victory and usually applies only to things (a *triumphal* procession). *Triumphant* is victorious or successful or exulting in success or victory and usually applies only to people (the *triumphant* champions).

The troupe entertained the troops.

troop, troupe   A *troop* is a body of people, such as a military or Boy Scout unit. *Troops* usually refers to a group of soldiers and is often used figuratively, in a reference to an office staff, for example. (Nice job, *troops!*) A *trooper* is a cavalryman or mounted police officer or, in some states, a state police officer. A *troupe* is a group of actors, dancers, singers, etc. A *trouper* is a member of a touring theatrical company or a veteran actor.

true   Its principal preposition is *to* (*true to* form, *true to* their word). Sometimes it takes *for*. (The same is *true for* most other students.)

true facts   usually redundant. Omit *true*.

trust   The verb takes the prepositions *in* and *to*. (*Trust to* luck. *Trust in* God.) The noun uses *in*. (Put your *trust in* the bank.)

trustee, trusty   A *trustee* is someone appointed, often to a board, to administer the affairs of a company, institution, etc., or a person who holds title to property for the benefit of another. A *trusty* is a convict who is considered trustworthy and is granted special privileges. The plurals are *trustees* and *trusties*. *Trustees* is sometimes used in reference to *trusties*, an error.

try and   *Try and* is an idiom acceptable to most commentators and dictionaries in speech and casual writing. (*Try and* make me. *Try and* stop me. *Try and* call her tonight.) In more serious contexts, *try to* should be used. (*Try to* finish the job this week. They *tried to* reach the far shore by dark.)

turbid, turgid   *Turbid* means clouded, opaque, muddy, confused, obscure (*turbid* water). *Turgid* means swollen, distended, inflated, overblown, pompous, bombastic (*turgid* river, a *turgid* explanation).

U

ultimatum The plural *ultimatums* is preferred over *ultimata*.

umbrella See PARASOL, UMBRELLA.

unalienable, inalienable If you're quoting the Declaration of Independence, it's "certain *unalienable* rights." Otherwise, it's *inalienable*.

unaware, unawares *Unaware* is an adjective (*unaware* of the problem). *Unawares* is an adverb (catch someone *unawares*). *Unaware* also is used as an adverb, but not as often as *unawares*.

unbeknown, unbeknownst Both are recognized as standard terms meaning without one's knowledge and are used equally. (*Unbeknownst* [or *unbeknown*] to me, Helen called off the party.)

unbelief See DISBELIEF, UNBELIEF.

unbend, unbending To *unbend* is to relax, unwind, become less tense. (They had a beer to *unbend* after leaving the office.) *Unbending* means unyielding, rigid, inflexible. (They were *unbending* in their opposition to the project.)

undertaker See MORTICIAN.

under way See WAY, WEIGH.

uneatable See INEDIBLE, UNEATABLE.

unequal Its preposition is *to* (*unequal to* the task).

unhuman See INHUMAN, UNHUMAN.

uninterested See DISINTERESTED, UNINTERESTED.

unique While the battle still rages over the status of this word as an absolute, meaning "having no equal, unparalleled," most dictionaries have broadened their definitions to include "not typical, unusual, remarkable." Most dictionaries and commentators agree that such modifiers as more, very, most, quite, rather, nearly, and somewhat should not be used in the unparalleled sense but are acceptable for the unusual sense.

unknown Do not use *unknown* when what you mean is unidentified or undisclosed (the body of an *unknown* man). (Unidentified.) (She left for an *unknown* destination.) (Undisclosed.)

unorganized, disorganized *Unorganized* means not organized, lacking order and unity. (The firm's new office was *unorganized*.) *Disorganized* applies to an existing organization that has been disrupted or put in disarray, thrown into confusion. (The unexpected development left their office *disorganized*.)

unprecedented having no precedent or parallel. It should not be used when you mean uncommon or remarkable. (The swimmer's performance in the Olympics was *unprecedented*.)

unqualified, disqualified *Unqualified* means lacking the required qualifications (*unqualified* for the job) or not modified, without reservations or restrictions (*unqualified* acceptance). *Disqualified* means rendered ineligible, unfit, deprived of rights or privileges. (The athlete was *disqualified* for using drugs.)

unravel See RAVEL, UNRAVEL.

unsatisfied, dissatisfied *Unsatisfied* usually means short of satisfaction, short of expectations. (The small sandwich left my hunger *unsatisfied*.) *Dissatisfied* also means not satisfied, but in the sense of discontented, displeased, offended. (I was *dissatisfied* with the painters' work.)

until See TILL, UNTIL.

up accepted by most recent dictionaries as a verb meaning increase or raise. (Let's *up* the ante. They *upped* their prices.)

upward, upwards *Upward* is preferred as an adverb (moving *upward*); as an adjective it is the only form that can modify a following noun (*upward* trend).

upwards of   Both *upwards of* and *upward of* may be used for "more than," although *upwards of* is more common. (The fund campaign raised *upwards of* $200,000.)

used to   Past tense of *use* is used with *to* to indicate a former state, practice, or custom. (I *used to* live in that house.) When did is used, the construction is *use to*. (*Didn't* you *use to* live in that house?)

useful   Depending on the context, it uses the prepositions *to* (This will be *useful to* me.), *for* (The calculator will be *useful for* balancing my checkbook.), and *in* (The map will be *useful in* finding our way.).

usual, customary   *Usual* applies to what is normal, ordinary, expected on the basis of previous experience (my *usual* cup of coffee). *Customary* refers to something that is in accord with the practices, conventions, or usages of the community, a group, or an individual. (In our house, it was *customary* to say grace before dinner.)

V

valuable, valued   *Valuable* means having great material or monetary value, being of great use or service (a *valuable* painting, *valuable* information). *Valued* is highly regarded, much esteemed (a *valued* friend), or appraised (*valued* at less than a hundred dollars). *Valuable* is also used in the sense of highly regarded (a *valuable* friend).

vary   Its chief preposition is *from*. (This year's play *varied* considerably *from* last year's.) Sometimes it is followed by *with*. (Sales *vary with* the time of year.)

V-E Day, V-J Day   *V-E Day*: May 8, 1945, the day Germany's surrender was announced in World War II. Two dates are given for *V-J Day*: August 14, 1945, the day fighting with Japan ended in World War II, or September 2, 1945, the day the Japanese surrender was formally signed. Note the hyphens. The initials stand for Victory in Europe and Victory over Japan.

venal, venial   *Venal* is susceptible to bribery or corruption, characterized by corruption (a *venal* judge, a *venal* agreement). *Venial* means easily excused or forgiven (a *venial* omission).

verbiage   *Verbiage* applies to words in excess of those needed for clarity—*wordiness*, in other words. *Excess verbiage* is redundant. *Verbiage* also may refer to the manner of expressing oneself in speech or writing.

After the lecture, George cleaned up the verbiage.

vest   Its prepositions are *in* and *with*. (The court *vested* the power of attorney in Jones. Jones was *vested with* the power of attorney.)

veto   The tenses are *vetoes, vetoed, vetoing*. The plural is *vetoes*.

via   Its principal meaning is by way of. (I went from Miami to Chicago *via* Atlanta.) It is not incorrect to use *via* to mean by means of, through, or by the medium or agency of. (The package was shipped *via* parcel post.)

vice, vise   A *vice* is an immoral or evil practice or habit. (I developed my *vices* early.) A *vise* is a clamping tool with jaws to hold an object being worked on. In British English, *vice* is the form used for both senses.

vicious circle   a chain of events in which the solution to a problem creates a new problem and aggravates the original difficulty. It is sometimes called a *vicious cycle*.

vie   usually followed by *with* or *for*. (Yale *vied with* Harvard. Yale and Harvard *vied for* the championship.)

view   *With a view* is usually followed by *to*, though *with a view of* or *toward* occasionally appears. *With a view to* is almost always followed by a participle rather than an infinitive. (I studied hard *with a view to* graduating early.)

villain   A slip of the keyboard could give you *villian*.

violin   See FIDDLE, VIOLIN.

virtually   See PRACTICALLY, VIRTUALLY.

visit   In the sense of chat or converse, *visit* is usually followed by the preposition *with*. (I *visited with* John for a couple of hours today.) One dictionary considers this use colloquial and another informal. Others treat it as standard.

vocation   See AVOCATION, VOCATION.

void   Its preposition is *of* (*void of* meaning).

Volkswagen   The name of the German auto maker is often misspelled *Volkswagon*.

vulnerable   takes the preposition *to* (*vulnerable to* attacks from both sides).

W

wacky   This spelling is preferred to *whacky* for this slang term that means irrational, eccentric, or crazy.

wait for, wait on   *Wait on* means to serve, as in "I *waited on* customers in a diner." It is standard English in this sense. It is in widespread usage in place of *wait for* in the sense of *await*, as in "I'm *waiting on* the bus," but most dictionaries and usage guides advise us to avoid this in general usage. See AWAIT, WAIT.

waive, wave   Sometimes confused. To *waive* is to relinquish, refrain from, forgo, give up. (They *waived* the extradition hearing.) To *wave* is to move back and forth or up and down (flags *waving* in the breeze).

waiver, waver   A *waiver* is the act of relinquishing a right, claim, or privilege or a document showing this. (We decided to forgo the preliminary hearing and signed the *waiver*.) To *waver* is to show irresolution or indecision, to vacillate, to weave or flicker. (When it came time to take the final step, I *wavered*.)

warn   The use of *warn* as an intransitive verb is acceptable. (The company *warned* against using the unlighted parking lot at night. The signal *warns* of approaching trains.)

wary   most often followed by the preposition *of*. (Be *wary of* dragons.)

wax, wane   To *wax* is to increase in strength, intensity, numbers, etc. (I noticed displeasure *waxing* among the people.) and to grow or become. (The speaker *waxed* sentimental.) To *wane* is to decrease gradually in size, amount, intensity, or degree. (My interest is *waning*.) Applied to the moon, *wax* refers to a gradual increase in the illuminated area between the new moon and the full moon, and *wane* refers to the reverse.

way   *Way* is frequently used as an adverb to mean at a great distance, to a considerable extent, far (*way* back in 1950, *way* below the going price, *way* over there). Most dictionaries consider this use colloquial, informal, or regional.

ways widely used for *way* in the sense of distance but not advisable for serious usage (a long *ways* to go).

way, weigh A ship's crew *weighs anchor* (raises it) in preparation for getting *under way* (not *under weigh*). An anchor is *aweigh* when it has been raised just clear of the bottom. Two words is the preference for *under way*.

wean To *wean* in its literal sense is to end dependence on a mother's milk. In its figurative sense it is to cause someone to give up something, such as a habit or some other interest (*weaned* from cigarettes, *weaned* off nightly poker games). It is widely used to mean to raise or bring up on, to become accustomed to from an early age, but this sense is criticized by usage authorities and not recognized in some dictionaries, although a couple present it as standard (*weaned* on police work).

weave In its literal senses, *wove* and *woven* are the past tense and past participle. (They *wove* baskets. They have *woven* many garments.) This is also true in most figurative senses (*wove* a story of suspense), except the past tense and participle become *weaved* when the reference is to a winding course or a side-to-side motion. (I *weaved* through traffic. I have *weaved* through this course many times.)

weird not *wierd*.

well See GOOD, WELL.

well-nigh almost, nearly. It is treated as standard by recent dictionaries. (It's *well-nigh* bedtime. The task was *well-nigh* impossible.)

Welsh rabbit, rarebit *Welsh rabbit* is preferred to *Welsh rarebit* for the melted cheese dish. *Welsh rarebit* is considered the product of folk etymology.

Welsh, welch *Welsh* is the proper spelling for the noun and adjective pertaining to Wales and its people, language, and culture, as well as the verb meaning to fail to pay a debt or to go back on one's word (*welshed* on a bet). *Welch* also is used infrequently for the verb (*welched* on the agreement) but is rarely used for the noun and adjective that apply to the people of Wales. *Welsher* is also the better term for the one who does the welshing.

Westminster   It's *Westminster* (not *Westminister*) for the abbey and the borough of London and the sites that bear their name.

whatever   preferred as one word, not two. It is acceptable as an interrogative. (*Whatever* did you mean by that?) It should not be followed by *that* in such constructions as "We disputed *whatever* claims that [omit] our opponents had made." It is often used at the end of a series to mean whatnot, anything else of that sort (goats, cows, or *whatever*) with *or* frequently omitted. This construction has a few critics.

whence   See HENCE, WHENCE.

whereabouts   usually singular, but it may become plural when more than one location is involved. (The mayor's *whereabouts* is a mystery. One crew headed north and the other one went south, and their current *whereabouts* are unknown.)

whether or not   Usually *or not* is not necessary, but look at your construction carefully before deciding whether it is dispensable. (We'll decide tomorrow *whether* to fly [*or not* isn't needed]. We'll go whether it rains or not [*or not* is necessary].)

which   See THAT, WHICH.

wholly   often misspelled.

whose, who's   These two words are very often confused. *Whose* is a possessive pronoun. *Who's* is a contraction for *who is* or *who has*. (*Whose* deal is it? *Who's* dealing?)

-wise   Long accepted when it means "in the manner or direction of" (*clockwise, lengthwise, crabwise*), -*wise* meaning "with regard to" (*moneywise, pricewise, percentagewise*) is rejected by most critics and dictionaries.

withhold   The double *h* confuses some people.

witness   The verb applies to an act, event, or occurrence but not a person or thing. You may witness a ball game or an accident or a wedding (We *witnessed* an accident.) but not a tree or a hill or a highway. (We *witnessed* a beautiful maple.)

Mary went to the gym
at 5, as was her wont.

wont The adjective, meaning accustomed or inclined, is followed by an infinitive. (Harry went to the bar at five o'clock, as he was *wont* to do.) The noun means custom, habit, practice. (Mary went to the gym at five, as was her *wont*.) Don't confuse *wont* with *won't*.

woolly preferred spelling.

Workers' compensation The apostrophe falls after the *s*, not before: *workers'*, not *worker's*.

worst It's "if *worst* comes to *worst*" or "if the *worst* comes to the *worst*," not "if worse comes to *worst*."

would of See SHOULD OF.

wrack See NERVE-RACKING and RACK, WRACK.

wretch See RETCH, WRETCH.

wreak, wreck Havoc is *wreaked*, not *wrecked*, as it often appears, nor is it *wrought*, which is the past tense and past participle of *work*.

wrong, wrongly Generally, when the two are used as adverbs, *wrongly* is used before the word it modifies and *wrong* follows it, although *wrongly* is also used sometimes after the word (the *wrongly* accused official, the official was accused *wrongly*, the word was spelled *wrong*).

wrought See WREAK, WRECK.

X

Xmas   considered objectionable even though it has been around since the middle of the sixteenth century. The *X* represents the Greek letter *chi*, the first letter of *Christo*, the Greek word for *Christ*.

Y

yearn   most often follows the preposition *for* (*yearning for* the good old days).

you-all   means *you* and is used in addressing two or more persons or one person who represents others. This is heard chiefly in the southern United States. The contraction is *y'all*.

your   often used casually in the sense of *a, an,* or *the.* (She's not *your* run-of-the-mill mathematics professor.)

yours   does not take an apostrophe (as in *your's*).

your, you're   *Your* is a possessive pronoun (Here is *your* book.) and *you're* is the contraction of *you are.* (*You're* the greatest.)

Z

zero   As the plural, *zeros* is preferred over *zeroes*.

ZIP code   Capitalize *ZIP*. It stands for *Zone Improvement Program*.